Es tials for Successful
English Language
Teaching

Essentials for Successful English Language Teaching

Thomas S. C. Farrell and
George M. Jacobs

continuum

Continuum International Publishing Group

The Tower Building
11 York Road
London SE1 7NX

80 Maiden Lane
Suite 704, New York
NY 10038

© Thomas S. C. Farrell and George M. Jacobs 2010

Thomas S. C. Farrell and George M. Jacobs have asserted their right under the Copyright, Designs and Patents Act, 1988, to be identified as the Authors of this work.

British Library Cataloguing-in-Publication Data
A catalogue record for this book is available from the British Library.

ISBN: 978-1-8470-6441-7 (hardback)
      978-1-8470-6442-4 (paperback)

Library of Congress Cataloging-in-Publication Data
A catalog record is available from the Library of Congress

Typeset by Newgen Imaging Systems Pvt Ltd, Chennai, India
Printed and bound in Great Britain by
CPI Antony Rowe, Chippenham, Wiltshire

Contents

Acknowledgments

By writing this book we acknowledge that we are standing on the shoulders of giants and we are really only fine tuning what the giants of our field have already postulated. In particular we are grateful for the mentorship of Professor Jack Richards who encouraged us to write a paper on this topic earlier (Jacobs & Farrell, 2003) and his overall contribution to the understanding of communicative language teaching (with Ted Rogers). In addition, we would like to acknowledge the contributions of all the professionals and students we both have met during our careers that made writing this book possible, as well as the patience both our families have shown us.

About the Authors

Thomas S. C. Farrell is Professor of Applied Linguistics at Brock University, Canada. His professional interests include Reflective Practice, and Language Teacher Education and Development. He is the series editor for the Language Teacher Research series (Asia, Americas, Africa, Australia/New Zealand, Europe, and the Middle East) for TESOL, USA. His recent books are *Succeeding with English language learners: A guide for beginning teachers* (2006, Corwin Press, Sage Publications); *What successful literacy teachers do: 70 research-based strategies for teachers, reading coaches, and instructional planners* (2007, co-authored with Neal Glasgow, Corwin Press, Sage Publications); *Reflective language teaching: From research to practice* (2007, Continuum Press); and *Teaching reading to English language learners: A reflective guide* (2008, Corwin Press, Sage Publications).

George M. Jacobs is a consultant with JF New Paradigm Education in Singapore. His interests include cooperative learning and global issues. He is on the executive board of the International Association for the Study of Cooperation in Education (http://www.iasce.net) and co-edits the newsletter of the TESOLers for Social Responsibility caucus of Teachers of English to Speakers of Other Languages (http://www.tesolers4sr.org).

Preface

Education is meant to open magical doors to students, offer exciting, fulfilling careers for teachers, and help create a world in which people work together for the common good. The possibilities are great. Students have so much to learn and so many ways to learn it. Similarly, we teachers have so much to learn about what we teach and the fascinatingly complex paths to facilitating student learning. **Essentials for Successful English Language Teaching** is about how we teach second language (mostly English as a Second Language (ESL) and English as a Foreign Language (EFL)) and how our second language students learn. "There's nothing as practical as a good theory" (Kurt Lewin, 1951, p. 169) probably best sums up how we arranged the contents of this book (see also Chapter 10) as we think it is a practical approach to teaching second language yet, all the activities are backed up solidly with clearly explained theories about where they came from.

Essentials for Successful English Language Teaching is about helping second language teachers maintain and rediscover the reasons that led them to take up teaching, reasons such as sharing their love of learning, making the world a better place, and working together with students and colleagues toward common goals. We strongly believe that the ideas in this book can create excitement, joy, and satisfaction among second language teachers and their students. What we maintain is that the ideas we've gathered and attempt to illuminate in this book bring with them the hope of many days in which an inner smile tells us teachers that, yes, we made the right choice when we chose this profession. **Essentials for Successful English Language Teaching** takes a 'big picture' view of second language learning and teaching. The eight essentials presented in this book are interwoven with each other, so that they are best implemented as a whole, rather than one at a time. Each supports the other; each is best understood as a big picture, rather than as individual puzzle pieces. Chapter 1 outlines in detail what the book is about and what is included in each chapter.

How to use this book

This book consists of ten chapters, eight of which detail all essentials plus the introduction and final chapters that offer final reflections on the use of the essentials. The eight chapters that look in detail at each of these eight essentials start from Chapter 2 and end at Chapter 9. The parts of each of these eight essentials in these chapters include the following:

- A brief story in each chapter that places the chapter's theme in a real-life context
- A short explanation of the basics of the chapter's theme. This also includes the theoretical foundations of the concept – theories and theoreticians whose works are often cited
- Classroom implications – the activities and learning environment that are congruent with the chapter theme. This is the main section in each chapter.
- Roles of teachers
- Roles of students
- Conclusion
- Reflections of each chapter that include questions and tasks

Writing this book has brought us (the two authors) a better understanding of why these eight essentials in second language education are, indeed, essential, and this has given us a great sense of urgency about seeing them implemented within the communicative language teaching approach to second language education. We hope that you our readers will carefully consider the ideas we present and that you will then form your own opinions and take your own paths, along with colleagues, students, and other voyagers, on the wide, wondrous, and sometimes wild journey that is second language education.

Essentials for Successful English Language Teaching

1

Chapter Outline

Introduction

Since the 1970s communicative language teaching has been one of the most popular teaching methodologies around the world in second language education. Before that, the more traditional teaching methods (e.g., Audio-Lingual Method; Grammar-Translation Method) that were employed focused more on producing accurate, grammatically correct target language. Communicative Language Teaching (CLT) however began to change the emphasis to where learners produce the language with a focus on fluency and where errors are seen as being a part of development. In traditional classes, teachers were seen as the knowledge providers and sole controllers of the class. In the approach English language teachers share this control and "facilitate" learning rather than dispense knowledge. So CLT represents a major change and is considered one of the main approaches to second language education today (Richards, 2005). Jacobs and Farrell (2001, 2003) label this major change in teaching and learning a second language a *paradigm shift* because in order to successfully implement the CLT approach we must shift our thinking about teachers, students, learning, and teaching a second language. The idea of the shift in focus is illustrated by the story of the "Cricket and the Coin."

One pleasant summer day at lunch time two colleagues, A and B, were walking along a busy street in Atlanta when A turned to B and said, "Do you hear that cricket across the street?" to which B replied, "How could I possibly hear a cricket with all this traffic." Her colleague confidently said, "Let's cross the street and I'll show you." They carefully made their way through the traffic to a flower box on the other side where, sure enough, there was a cricket. B was astounded. "How could you hear a little cricket amid all this noise? You must have super-human hearing!" "The key," A explained, "is not how well we hear but what we listen for." To illustrate, she took a coin from her purse, threw it in the air, and let it drop on the sidewalk. Soon, the sound of braking vehicles filled the air, as cars came to a halt. Drivers and pedestrians turned to look for the rattling coin. As A reached to retrieve her coin, B smiled and said, "Now, I see what you mean; it's all a matter of focus."

This chapter outlines and describes eight essentials of second language education that fit with the CLT paradigm shift. The subsequent eight chapters of this book then focus on one of the eight essentials and the final chapter concludes the discussion. These eight essentials are: encourage Learner Autonomy, emphasize the Social Nature of Learning, develop Curricular Integration, Focus on Meaning, celebrate Diversity, expand Thinking Skills, utilize Alternative Assessment methods, and promote English language Teachers as Co-learners. We argue that in second language education, although the CLT paradigm shift was initiated many years ago, it really has been only partially implemented. Two reasons for this partial implementation are: (1) by trying to understand each essential separately, second language educators have weakened their understanding by missing the larger picture; and (2) by trying to implement each essential separately, second language educators have made the difficult task of shift or change even more challenging. We now give a brief orientation to CLT and how we should really understand and implement it as a real paradigm shift.

Communicative language teaching

CLT can be seen as a set of "principles about the goals of language teaching, how learners learn a language, the kinds of classroom activities that best facilitate learning, and the roles of teachers and learners in the class-room" (Richards, 2005, p. 1). CLT has been the "in" approach to second language education since its beginning in the early 1970s, and has now become the driving force that affects the planning, implementation, and evaluation of English Language Teaching (ELT) throughout the world (Richards & Rodgers, 2001). That said, not many English language teachers or second language educators are in agreement or even clear in their own minds as to what exactly CLT is, and there exist as many diverse interpretations as there are language teachers and second language educators. This wide variation in implementation of CLT is not, as we discuss in the chapter on celebrating Diversity, necessarily a bad thing. Rather, it is a natural product of the range of contexts in which second language learning takes place and the range of experiences that students, teachers, and other stakeholders bring with them.

In its early inception CLT was seen as an approach to teaching English as a second or foreign language for the purposes of enabling second language learners to be able to use language functionally, meaningfully and appropriately, instead of the previous emphasis on correctness (e.g., Finocchiaro & Brumfit, 1983). However, over the years ESL and EFL teachers have interpreted a CLT approach to language teaching in many different ways with many thinking that the teacher just forms groups in their classes and let the students practice speaking the second language. The end result that teachers using this approach were seeking was that their students become competent in speaking that second language. Richards (2005) calls this *phase 1* of the CLT movement and he says it continued until the late 1960s. In phase 1 the previous traditional approaches that gave priority to grammatical competence as a foundation for language proficiency gave way to functional and skill-based teaching that had a "fluency over accuracy" pedagogical purpose. The next phase of CLT according to Richards (2005) was the classic CLT period from the 1970s to the 1990s.

In this phase, the place of grammar in instruction was questioned because it seemed to result only in grammatical competence that produced grammatically correct sentences under controlled conditions but did not, according to many, improve oral production or aid the communicative use of language. So what was really called for at that time was communicative competence where students could actually communicate orally in the second language; for example, Hymes (1972) suggested that Chomsky's ideal native speaker with linguistic competence include the sociolinguistic component of communicative competence of *knowledge of* and *ability for* language use with respect to four factors: "possibility, feasibility, appropriateness and accepted usage" (p. 19). More recently, Richards (2005, p. 1) suggests that communicative competence includes the following aspects of language knowledge:

- knowing how to use language for a range of different purposes and functions
- knowing how to vary our use of language according to the setting and the participants (e.g. knowing when to use formal and informal speech or when to use language appropriately for written as opposed to spoken communication)
- knowing how to produce and understand different types of texts (e.g. narratives, reports, interviews, conversations)
- knowing how to maintain communication despite having limitations in one's language knowledge (e.g. through using different kinds of communication strategies).

Since the 1990s CLT has continued to evolve by drawing from different educational paradigms and diverse sources with the result that as Richards (2005, p. 24) maintains, there is still "no single or agreed upon set of practices that characterize current communicative language teaching." Rather, he suggests that communicative language teaching these days refers to "a set of generally agreed upon principles that can be applied in different ways, depending on the teaching context, the age of the learners, their level, their learning goals." In addition, Brown (2000) has maintained that CLT should include the following:

- Classroom goals are focused on all the components of communicative competence and not restricted to grammatical or linguistic competence.
- Language techniques are designed to engage learners in the pragmatic, authentic, functional use of language for meaningful purposes.
- Fluency and accuracy are seen as complementary principles underlying communicative techniques.
- In the communicative classroom, students ultimately have to use the language, productively and receptively, in unrehearsed contexts. (p. 266)

Richards (2005) maintains that if we ask ESL/EFL teachers today who say they follow the CLT approach what exactly they do, or what they mean by "communicative," their explanations will vary widely, from an absence of grammar in a conversation course, to a focus on open-ended discussion activities. In our view, the key problem lies in the fact that not enough teachers are implementing CLT and some of those who do implement it have done so too infrequently, too often returning to the traditional paradigm. Later in this chapter, we examine reasons for this.

Understanding communicative language teaching

In second language education, the CLT paradigm shift over the past 40 years, which Long (1997) likens to a revolution, flows from the positivism to post-positivism shift in science (see also Chapter 10) and involves a move away from the tenets of behaviorist psychology and structural linguistics and toward cognitive, and later, socio-cognitive psychology and more contextualized, meaning-based views of language. Key components on this shift concern:

1. Focusing greater attention on the role of learners rather than the external stimuli learners are receiving from their environment. Thus, the center of attention shifts from the teacher to the student. This shift is generally known as the move from teacher-centered instruction to learner-centered or learning-centered instruction.
2. Focusing greater attention on the learning process rather than on the products that learners produce. This shift is known as a move from product-oriented instruction to process-oriented instruction.
3. Focusing greater attention on the Social Nature of Learning rather than on students as separate, decontextualized individuals.
4. Focusing greater attention on Diversity among learners and viewing these differences not as impediments to learning but as resources to be recognized, catered to, and appreciated. This shift is known as the study of individual differences.
5. In research and theory-building, focusing greater attention on the views of those internal to the classroom rather than solely valuing the views of those who come from outside to study classrooms, investigate and evaluate what goes on there, and engage in theorizing about it. This shift is associated with such innovations as qualitative research, which highlights the subjective and affective, the participants' insider views, and the uniqueness of each context.

6. Along with this emphasis on context comes the idea of connecting the school with the world beyond as a means of promoting holistic learning.
7. Helping students understand the purpose of learning and developing their own purposes.
8. A whole-to-part orientation instead of a part-to-whole approach. This involves such approaches as beginning with meaningful whole texts and then helping students understand the various features that enable the texts to function, e.g., the choice of words and the text's organizational structure.
9. An emphasis on the importance of meaning rather than drills and other forms of rote learning.
10. A view of learning as a life-long process rather than something done to prepare for an exam.

As mentioned earlier, the CLT paradigm shift in second language education is part of a larger shift that affected many other fields (See Voght, 2000 for a discussion of parallels between paradigm shifts in foreign language education at U.S. universities and paradigm shifts in education programs in business and other professions). Oprandy (1999) links trends in second language education with those in the field of city planning. He likens behaviorism's top-down, one-size-fits-all approach to education to a similar trend in city planning in which outside experts designed for uniformity and attempted to do away with Diversity. In response, a new paradigm arose in city planning, a bottom-up one that sought to zone for Diversity. Describing the current paradigm in second language education, Oprandy writes:

> The communicative approach requires a complexity in terms of planning and a tolerance for messiness and ambiguity as teachers analyze students' needs and design meaningful tasks to meet those needs. The pat solutions and deductive stances of audiolingual materials and pedagogy, like the grammar-translation texts and syllabi preceding them, are no longer seen as sensitive to students' needs and interests. Nor are they viewed as respectful of students' intelligence to figure things out inductively through engaging problem-solving and communicative tasks. (p. 44)

Another parallel that Oprandy draws between new ideas in city planning and new ideas in second language education have to do with the role of the subjective. In city planning, attention began to focus on people's need for a sense of security and belonging in people-centered cities. These concerns, as Oprandy suggests, are matched in second language education by the desire to facilitate an atmosphere in which students are willing to take risks, to admit mistakes, and to help one another.

Implementing communicative language teaching

The CLT paradigm shift in second language education outlined above has led to many suggested changes in how English as a second/foreign language teaching is conducted and conceived (Richards & Rodgers, 2001). Our objective in writing this book is to argue that the CLT paradigm shift has not been implemented as widely or as successfully as it might have been because English language educators and other stakeholders have tried to understand and implement the shift in a piecemeal rather than a holistic manner. Thus, we suggest that English as a second/foreign language educators consider eight major changes associated with this shift because of the impact they already have had on the language education field and for the potential impact they could have if they were used in a more integrated fashion.

We selected these eight because we see them as essential, still in progress, and interlinked with one another. By helping to promote the understanding and use of these eight elements, we hope this book will provide teachers with a handy, user-friendly resource. Certainly, other related elements of good learning and teaching also deserve attention.

First, we briefly explain each essential (we later devote a whole chapter to each essential), explore links between the essential and the larger paradigm shift and look at various second language classroom implications and then we devote an individual chapter to each essential. These eight essentials are:

1. Encourage Learner Autonomy
2. Emphasize Social Nature of Learning
3. Develop Curricular Integration
4. Focus on Meaning
5. Celebrate Diversity
6. Expand Thinking Skills
7. Utilize Alternative Assessment Methods
8. Promote English Language Teachers as Co-learners.

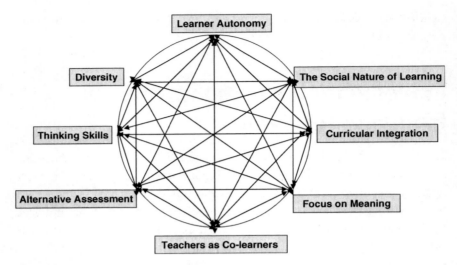

Figure 1.1 Eight essentials for successful second language teaching

Figure 1.1 provides an illustration of the interdependence of these eight essentials of the paradigm shift in second language education. The circular nature of the figure emphasizes that all the changes are parts of a whole and that the successful implementation of one is dependent on the successful implementation of others.

This book focuses on these eight essentials in second language education, the links between the eight, and, most importantly, how these essentials are being used and can be implemented. We hope this book contributes in some small way to encouraging fuller development of these and related essentials. The eight essentials are briefly explained as follows.

Learner autonomy

Within a CLT approach to second language education we focus more on the role of learners rather than the external stimuli learners receive from their environment, such as from teachers and materials. In other words, the center of attention in learning English as a second/foreign language has shifted from the teacher and materials (the external) to the student (the internal). This shift is generally known as the move from teacher-centered instruction to learner (or student)-centered instruction. Learner Autonomy is a key concept here: learners have an important share of the responsibility for and control over their own learning. Chapter 2 outlines this first essential in CLT in more detail.

The social nature of learning

As the name suggests, to be social in learning we mean some form of interaction and cooperation is necessary within a CLT approach to second language education. We focus greater attention on the Social Nature of Learning English as a second/foreign language rather than on students as separate, decontextualized individuals. To understand and promote learning, we look not only at individuals but also at the people who make up their world and the connections between them. These people include not only teachers but also peers and others such as administrators and people in the outside community. Cooperation is valued over competition without excluding the latter completely. When students collaborate they all play leadership roles. Chapter 3 outlines this essential in CLT in more detail.

Curricular integration

Curricular Integration refers to a second language pedagogical approach which fuses knowledge from different disciplines to create more meaningful contexts for overall learning. The traditional fragmentation of content by disciplines assumes that students will recognize the links between the disciplines on their own, but this can be difficult for second language students whose main focus may be the language rather than the content. However, with a CLT approach to teaching and learning English as a second/foreign language the integrated approach purposefully and systematically guides second language students toward discovering these connections and processes; connections and processes that help ESL/EFL students better understand themselves and the world around them. In the highest form, this student-centered approach uses real-life issues and varied resources to bring students as close to the "real thing" as possible. Furthermore, integration can also include integrating the various language skills, as well as integrating the academic with the social and emotional. Chapter 4 outlines this essential in CLT in more detail.

Focus on meaning

For this essential we focus on learning English as a second/foreign language for purposes other than just passing an exam. Education is not just preparation for life; it is also participation in life. Students understand the purposes of learning and develop their own purposes for learning regardless of the subject. Within learning English as a second/foreign language we suggest that understanding also involves our students' comprehension of what they are learning rather than learning by rote learning methods such as drills so that they can be educated as complete human beings. Chapter 5 explains this essential in a CLT approach to second language education in more detail.

Diversity

First of all, we celebrate Diversity among our second language learners and we see this diversity as a plus in our English as a second/foreign language classes. We focus on discerning, taking into account, and appreciating differences among our second language learners within a CLT approach to language education; thus we consider all second language (indeed all students) to be unique. This uniqueness includes differences not only in first language backgrounds, but also in intelligence profile, personality, and such other background factors as race, ethnicity, social class, religion, sex, and sexual preference. We suggest in this CLT concept that no standard, one-size-fits-all way of teaching a second language exists, and that differences of opinion and perspective offer opportunities for learning rather than being cause for winner-take-all conflict. Chapter 6 outlines this essential in CLT in more detail.

Thinking skills

For this CLT essential we focus on how students learn by a process of expanding their Thinking Skills rather than looking only at what they produce. This emphasis on process rather than just on end-product encourages second language students and teachers to promote reflection on one's thinking, to encourage deeper critical thinking, and more varied ways of solving problems, and to gain sense of greater questioning of how things are done. With an appreciation of the complexity, uncertainty, nonlinearity, and instability of knowledge in learning a second language, students not only come to see change as a constant but also that learning a second language (and learning in general) is a life-long process; indeed, we suggest that disruption and surprise are to be welcomed while learning. Chapter 7 outlines this essential in CLT in more detail.

Alternative assessment

We should point out immediately that when we say alternative we are not "throwing out the baby with the bathwater" because we still see the place of more traditional testing; it is just that now we want to suggest that English as a second/foreign language teachers and administrators take into account that not all our second language learners may respond to such testing in a manner that compliments their different cultural backgrounds and that we have alternative means of assessment that may be more suitable. So within a CLT approach to second language education we recognize that while standardized, objective-item tests do provide relevant information, sole reliance on such measures blinds us to a great deal of what is important in education. We suggest that more Alternative Assessments connect closely with real world purposes. Furthermore, this type of assessment is done not mainly by outsiders but more importantly by those actually in the classroom (peers) who grasp the particular context in all its complexity. Thus Alternative Assessment includes students assessing themselves, peers, and the "how" and "what" of their English as a second/foreign language learning. Additionally, Alternative Assessment focuses on what second language students can do rather than on what they cannot do. Chapter 8 outlines this essential in more detail.

Teachers as co-learners

The final concept within the eight essentials for successful implementation of CLT focuses on language teachers not principally as possessors of knowledge that is to be passed on to students; instead, teachers learn along with second language students because knowledge is dynamic and learning is a life-long process. Teachers learn with their students, and they learn along with their fellow teachers. Based on this learning, teachers join students in playing a greater role in such matters as materials design and institutional governance. Chapter 9 outlines this concept in more detail.

Eight essentials for successful English language teaching

Figure 1.1, shown earlier, suggests that the eight essential changes (outlined and discussed in more detail in subsequent chapters) are related and connected to one another. For example, the Social Nature of Learning connects with Learner Autonomy because by working in groups second language students become less dependent on teachers and more interdependent with each other. Curriculum Integration is facilitated by student–student interaction because second language students can pool their energies and knowledge to take on cross-curricular projects. The Social Nature of Learning element fits with an emphasis on meaning, as groups provide an excellent forum for students to engage in meaningful communication in their second language. The Diversity element provides mutual support for the Social Nature of Learning when students form heterogeneous groups and use collaborative skills to bring out and value the ideas and experiences of all the group members.

The Social Nature of Learning also provides an excellent venue for the use of the Thinking Skills element, as second language students attempt to explain concepts and procedures to their groupmates, as groupmates give each other feedback, and as they debate the proper course of action. The Alternative Assessment element synergizes with the Social Nature of Learning in several ways. For instance, cooperative learning provides scope for peer assessment, and an emphasis on the development of collaborative skills calls for different methods to assess these skills. Finally, the elements of Teachers as Co-learners go together with the Social Nature of Learning for at least two reasons. First, teachers often work with colleagues to learn more about education, e.g., by conducting action research and otherwise discussing their classes. By collaborating with fellow teachers, teachers model collaboration for their students and convince themselves of its benefits. Second, because cooperative learning means that teachers talk less, it allows teachers to get off the stage some of the time and spend more time facilitating student learning as well as their own learning. One of the techniques for this facilitation is to take part along with students, thus encouraging teachers to learn more.

Teaching English as a second/foreign language

"Communicative Language Teaching" is probably the answer given most frequently when English as a second/foreign language teachers are asked what approach they use to teach in their own classes, what they think is most successful and indeed, what the most popular approach is used by most teachers today. Although we all assume that we have the same understanding about what successful English as a second/foreign language instruction and CLT means and that we all implement CLT in the same way, the reality is far from a unified understanding or implementation in most second language classrooms. In fact, what we have noticed is that there seems to be a great deal of variation between countries, institutions within the same country, and even classrooms within the same institution when it comes to definitions of successful language instruction, and that the so-called paradigm shift in second language instruction toward CLT seems to be gradual, evolutionary, and piecemeal. There seem to be several reasons for this slow evolution within second language education.

One reason may be that changing beliefs and behaviors takes time in education and elsewhere (Fullan, 2008). Lack of change may also be a result of the difficulty of translating theory into practical application. That is, new ideas need a great deal of work by practicing teachers for these ideas to be translated into everyday teaching routines. Furthermore, one teacher working alone has much less change power than do groups of educators, including administrators and school district staff working together. Another possible explanation stems from a lack of understanding of what CLT is and the resulting fact that it has often been presented in a piecemeal fashion, rather than as a whole. In other words, many ESL/EFL teachers may have just started practicing immediately those parts of the CLT approach that they learned and that seemed most congenially implemented given the constraints faced by an individual teacher without understanding what exactly the CLT approach means. So the point of this book has been to reignite the CLT fires and to argue that in order to implement CLT as a successful approach to English as a second/foreign language education, we must realize that it should take a holistic perspective which has two main implications.

1. First, the changes are *ALL* related.
2. Second, when we attempt to implement these changes, if we do so in a piecemeal fashion, selecting changes as if they were items on an a la carte menu, we lessen the chances of success.

Thus, these innovations all fit together, like the pieces in a pattern cut to make a jigsaw puzzle. Each piece supports the others, and each builds on the others as outlined in Figure 1.1 above.

Conclusion

In this chapter (and throughout this book) we have urged our fellow second language educators to take a big picture approach to the changes in our approach to understanding and implementing CLT. We have argued that many of these essential changes stem from a previous underlying paradigm shift toward CLT that continues today. By examining this shift and looking for connections between various changes in our field, these changes can be better understood. Most importantly, by attempting to implement change in a holistic way, the chances of success greatly increase. This point has been made countless times in works on systems theory by Senge (2000), Wheatley (2006), and others. However, it is much easier to state in theory than to implement in practice. Perhaps the best-known and most painful example of the failure to implement holistic change in second language education is that in many cases while teaching methodology has become more communicative, testing remains within the traditional paradigm, consisting of discrete items, lower-order thinking, and a focus on form rather than meaning (Brown, 2000). This creates a backwash effect that tends to pull teaching back toward the traditional paradigm, even when teachers and others are striving to go toward the new paradigm.

Second language education plays an ever more important role as globalization, for better or worse, marches forward. Perhaps this is where the eighth change we discussed, Teachers as Co-learners (see Chapter 9), plays the crucial role. Many people are drawn to work in second language education because they enjoy learning languages and want to share this joy with others. All the changes that have taken place in our field challenge us to continue learning about our profession and to share what we learn with others, including our colleagues, so that we can continue to help our field develop. We hope you enjoy reading the next eight chapters that detail the eight essential and interconnected changes that are necessary for successful English as a second/foreign language instruction.

Encourage Learner Autonomy

Vignette

John Jones, an ESL teacher in the USA just graduated with an MA TESL (Master of Arts, teaching English as a second language) and is eager to implement all that he had learned in his graduate TESL program. One of the most interesting aspects of this program according to John was the focus throughout on the learner, or "as opposed to having the teacher decide everything in class," as he stated, and the encouragement of Learner Autonomy "where they can move from learning the second language to using the second language to learn." To John this was liberating because he reflected that he had studied a second language (Spanish) in an environment where the teacher decided everything and never let the students practice speaking the language or write on their own without strict controls on how to speak and write. In addition, at the end of his Spanish as a Second Language learning program he really did not feel that he had developed real autonomy in his language learning because he had been so dependent on the teacher for direction. However, from what he had just learned in his MA TESL program John discovered that it may indeed be possible to allow and invite students into the learning process. So, in his ESL language classes he has instituted a policy of checking his students' first language background and culture so that he can learn and thus know more about each student. Next, he designs his lessons while taking this background knowledge into account as he tries to include his students' interests and ideas. In order to get this information he interviews each student and also includes questions about how and what they would like to study in terms of the topics they would be interested in talking and writing about. His students seem to like these interviews because they realize that John is taking an interest in each of them and that their ideas about the learning process really matter. He also encourages his students to look at themselves as learners and to discover which learning style suits them best and which learning strategies they can best manipulate while learning the second language. In order to steer his students toward eventual auton-omy in their learning of the second language John now includes pair-work and group-work activities where the students can practice the language together and not worry about making mistakes. In addition, John has encouraged his students to read daily newspapers and watch television as they are all learning English as a second language and these exercises will further strengthen their language learning with the inevitable result of becoming autonomous language learners. John also checks regularly throughout the semester that the students are enjoying their learning.

Our students learn a second language usually because they want to be able to communicate with others who use that language in their daily lives. So the idea of proposing that our students should eventually become autonomous in their learning is essential if we are to follow the CLT approach as outlined in the previous chapter because Learner Autonomy as it is discussed in this chapter emphasizes the role of the learner rather than the role of the teacher. In order to emphasize the role of the learner in our classes we first need to know something about who is in our class, the learners, and this is evident in John's approach to teaching (above) as he designs his lessons with knowledge of who his learners are (the students' backgrounds, learning styles, learning strategies, etc.) while also encouraging his students to focus on their own learning responsibilities outside the classroom by reading daily newspapers in English, watching television shows in English and thus encouraging Learner Autonomy. This chapter on the essential of Learner Autonomy within a CLT approach to second language education is the first of the eight essentials we talk about for second language learners, teachers, and administrators. We place it first because we feel it sets the tone for the whole book in that we see second language education as existing on a continuum where learners start as beginner second language learners being very much dependent on the teacher for help and guidance, but ultimately we want them to proceed to the other end of the continuum where they become independent of the teacher as they develop into autonomous learners. The following sections in this chapter explain what we mean by Learner Autonomy and then map out how it can be implemented in second language classrooms.

Learner autonomy

Modern theories of learning emphasize the key role that learners play in the success of education. This might seem obvious, but previously, teachers and materials were given pride of place. However, the focus now is on the learner and the learning process and processes (learning styles and learning strategies of *each* student) rather than the previous teacher-centered approach where endless drilling was said to produce some sort of rudimentary success in using the second language with the use of prescribed lessons and teacher-proof materials delivered by dubiously qualified "language teachers."

In this chapter we link Learner Autonomy to Csikszentmihalyi's (1990) work on flow, and Vygotsky's (1978) concept of self-regulation. For example, we agree with Csikszentmihalyi's conclusions that flow occurs when people do what they see as meaningful work, are intrinsically motivated, and have or are developing skill in the activities they are doing. In line with the work of the theorists above, the classroom can be taken as a site for democratic practices and this provides another rationale for learner-centered education. A key concept here is that of the hidden curriculum (the knowledge, values, and beliefs that schools present to students and others), not by what is explicitly being taught, but by the process in which the actual instruction takes place (Loporchio, 2006). The point being that if schools and society talk about democracy but classroom practices do not reflect this because they are overly autocratic, students may be less likely to know how to function in a democratic learner-centered setting or even how to insist on this method if they recognize that they are being denied this right.

To be *autonomous,* then, means that our second language learners need to be able to have some choice as to the *what* and the *how* of the curriculum we are teaching them and, at the same time, they should feel responsible for their own learning and for the learning of those with whom they interact. In second language education Learner Autonomy involves second language learners gaining awareness of their own ways of learning such as learning styles and learning strategies, so that they can utilize their strengths and work on their weaknesses (Benson, 2007; Nowlan, 2008). The latter focus on learner strategies is important in second language education because research has indicated that our students can actually learn how to successfully manipulate their own strategy use. However, the former focus on learning styles is more difficult to manipulate because it is within the nature of the learner himself or herself; in other words, learning style is the given. When we speak about autonomy, we should realize that intrinsic motivation also plays a central and important role because Learner Autonomy means that the teacher no longer shoulders the entire burden of running the classroom, with students taking on more rights and responsibilities for their own learning in a learner-centered approach to second language learning. In summary, when we talk about Learner Autonomy within a CLT approach we recognize that we should

- understand our second language learners' backgrounds, beliefs, needs, and interests
- take all these into account when designing and implementing the curriculum
- help our students recognize, understand, and manipulate their strengths and weaknesses, as well as the learning process itself
- offer our students as many choices as possible in and control over their own learning
- encourage enjoyment of the learning process
- attain Learner Autonomy so that they can continue learning long after they leave our classrooms.

The following section outlines how second language teachers can implement Learner Autonomy in their classrooms within an overall CLT approach to second language education.

Classroom implications

Learner Autonomy is sometimes misunderstood as referring only to learners being able to work alone. However, by first learning how to collaborate with their peers, learners can slowly discover how to move away from dependence on the teacher to independence with the ultimate realization of working alone on their learning. So, when we think of Learner Autonomy in general and learner-centeredness in particular we see second language classrooms where students are interacting a lot, not only with the teacher but also with each other. For example, the use of small groups, including pairs, represents one means of enhancing Learner Autonomy (Pagel, 2002; Please see the chapter on the element of the Social Nature of Learning for more on this).

Group activities help second language students harness that power and by doing so they build their pool of learning resources because they can receive assistance from peers, and not just from the teacher. For example, many classrooms use the TTT (Team Then Teacher) guideline. In other words, when students have a question, they first ask their groupmates. Only if none of them are able to help do students consult the teacher. Taking TTT a step further is 3 + 1 B4 T, i.e., if students' 3 groupmates cannot help, they then ask 1 more group before turning to the teacher.

A frequent difficulty when we encourage students to look to themselves and peers as resources is that students feel that only the teacher can help, that classmates know as little as they do, that students helping students is "the blind leading the blind." To put it another way, if Student A knows 0 and Student B knows 0, 0 + 0 might well equal −1, as students leave each other more confused and off course. Ways to make sure students do not lead each other astray in such arrangements include setting up groups that are heterogeneous as to language proficiency so that more proficient peers can help their less proficient group-mates, using tasks that are doable for students, highlighting instances when students do well and help each other, and creating information gaps so that students need to learn from each other.

Another means of implementing Learner Autonomy in second language education is the use of an extensive reading program to augment regular reading instruction (Kweon & Kim, 2008). Here, second language students are allowed to choose their own reading materials that match their interests (rather than the teacher's interests or the interests of the curriculum developers, as is the case in many classrooms) and their proficiency levels. The students also have the choice of changing their minds once they have started such reading because if students begin a book or a magazine and it does not seem the right one for them, they can switch to some other reading material that may hold more interest. The hope is that extensive reading will assist second language students to become autonomous learners and to develop an appreciation for the enjoyment and knowledge to be gained via reading in their second language (as well as their first). Thus encouraging them to make reading a life-long habit.

Self-assessment provides another general way for second language students to develop their sense of autonomous learning (Rivers, 2001). The idea here is for second language learners to develop their own internal criteria for the quality of their work, rather than being dependent on external evaluation, or evaluators (often the teacher), as the sole judge of their strengths and weaknesses. Developing these internal criteria enables learners to make informed decisions about how to move their learning forward. With self-assessment, second language students no longer have to wait for the teacher to tell them how well they are doing and what they need to do next, an essential aspect of developing Learner Autonomy. Yes, the teacher remains generally the more knowledgeable and experienced person in the classroom, but the goal is for students to move toward and perhaps even beyond, the teacher's level of competence. Placing value on learners' knowledge helps them feel more capable of playing a larger role in their own learning (for more details see Chapter 7 on Alternative Assessments) or as one second language teacher summed it all up so eloquently:

> I found this (the old paradigm) to be very true of my teaching style (at least early on) that was probably shaped by the teaching style that I was taught under, that being the Old Teaching paradigm. I believe that my style (and teaching as a whole) is moving toward the New Paradigm of teaching. I initially thought it was my job to take the knowledge that I had and fill my student's heads. I found teaching to be uneventful, passive, impersonal, and boring. Now my teaching has evolved into a partnership between students where we work together to construct knowledge. Knowledge sharing is a 2 way street. I have found that it takes more time to be a better teacher but that the payoff is much larger. It has become more enjoyable to see students develop their own unique selves and personal competencies.

More specifically, language teachers can encourage Learner Autonomy by implementing the following activities that can be adjusted to each particular student's and teacher's needs and context.

Student-selected reading

As already mentioned in the discussion on extensive reading above this type of activity hopes to develop a life-long reading habit for our second language students, a life-long reading habit that can be a vital element in life-long learning. The two main ways that educators can encourage a life-long reading habit are: being readers themselves and letting their students know about this fact by reading in class with them, and providing time for their students to read on their own in the same class; this can provide the role model motivation for our second language students to continue with this habit outside of class. When we say "read on their own," we also mean that they can read anything they like, and this can include fiction and even comic books, but it can also include non-fiction and can be related to any subject area if the teacher wants to focus on a particular subject. The point here is that reading extensively means that students come to learn the joy of reading that they may not have experienced when reading textbooks in their various courses in school. So if for example, they want to read Stephen King's work, we allow them to read it as extensive reading focuses on the act (and joy) of reading. Programs that promote independent reading enjoy colorful names such as SURF (Silent Independent Reading for Fun), DEAR (Drop Everything and Read), and DIRT (Daily Independent Reading and Thinking).

Teachers can play an encouraging role for their students by facilitating their extensive reading since just because we give them say 20 minutes in a class to read does not mean that they will suddenly read with sustained concentration for that period of time if they have not done this before. So teachers should tell their students that one main activity at the end of the period of extensive reading is discussions of what they have read during the semester. To be able to participate in these class discussions students will have to be able to tell their peers about what they have read. Consequently, Farrell (2008) suggests that second language students should keep a reading log of some sort about the material they are reading so that they can draw on that information when discussing aspects of the book they have read. Then each class member can be asked to work individually or in pairs or groups to complete any of the following activities:

- Write a reaction letter to the author of the book and ask questions about the book and give comments – what you liked and did not like.
- Make a movie. "The Movie Version" (Farrell, 2008) is an activity where students cast actors and draw a poster for a movie based on a book they have read. "The Movie Version" as one alternative to the "boring book report."
- Students can also make a poster for the "movie-of-the-book" and/or redesign and make a new book cover. Rather than a movie, students could also consider making a radio play from the story.

Self-assessment

As mentioned above in the general discussion on classroom implementation, in order for second language students to take more control of their own education, they need to not only decide on their learning goals, but they also need to know where they are at in relation to those self-selected goals. In other words, they should know how to monitor their own strengths and weaknesses. To do this and encourage Learner Autonomy, self-assessment should complement assessment by teachers and peers as a key part of how student progress is monitored. Examples of self-assessment include the following:

Checklists: Before students hand in any assignment they review their work using a checklist of desired characteristics. This checklist can be developed jointly by teachers and students prior to students beginning the assignment although a student-designed checklist would be best as it can tell the teacher what aspects of learning the student thinks important.

Group work: When working in a group, time can be spent on each student reflecting on and sharing about their contributions to the group and in discussing how each of them can be a better group participants. This reflection and discussion can be facilitated by an initial discussion that the whole class participates in, considering the collaboration skills and how each one can lead the group, i.e., distributed leadership, by promoting the group's success in whichever way they can.

Student course evaluations

Nowadays, especially at the tertiary level, student input about the quality of teachers and courses can have a powerful impact, especially on the careers of their teachers. While the role that these student evaluations should play is debatable, it seems clear that giving students a role in evaluation of the people with whom and the programs in which they learn offers a means of increasing students' control over their own learning. However, too often student evaluations tend to be summative – done at the end of a course, rather than formative – done during a course. So we suggest that teachers conduct student evaluations at different parts of the course because by seeking student input at various stages in a course, the teacher can show that what second language students say at these various points in the course can impact their entire learning environment. In fact, we could seek student input at the end of each lesson by asking our students four simple questions:

1. What was this class about?
2. What was easy for you to learn?
3. What was difficult for you to learn?
4. What changes would you suggest (if any)?

Even if we do not agree with the student suggestions and do not implement changes that our second language students suggest, the process itself provides an opportunity to dialogue with our students about why we teach the way we do. We maintain that this dialogue, apart from giving our students more practical knowledge and practice in using the second language they are learning at that time, also shows that we are listening to them.

Bring Your Own Piece (BYOP) jigsaw

In the standard Jigsaw technique, students begin in "Home Teams" of four members each. The teacher *gives* each team member a different piece of reading material on a related topic (students can choose these topics or leave it to the teacher). Students then leave their "Home Teams" and form small "Expert Teams" with their classmates who have the same piece of reading. They study their assigned piece in preparation for teaching it to their "Home Team" members. In BYOP *Jigsaw*, students *find* their own pieces. For instance, if the class reading is on the medical topic of AIDS, then one member of each "Home Team" might be charged with learning about its causes, another with the history of the illness, another with its treatment, and the fourth with learning all about its prevention. So before going to their "Expert Team," each student does some research on the topic. They then combine that with the research done by their fellow experts in order to prepare to join their "Home Team" members for discussion.

BYOP Jigsaw is an example of the use of student-generated materials (Lee, Mcloughlin, & Chan, 2008). Such materials include those that students have made themselves, such as stories they have written, oral or written recounts of experiences they have had, as well as materials students have found and brought to class, including lyrics of songs that they enjoy. Increasing access to the internet has greatly facilitated locating such materials. Indeed, electronic tools have also provided new opportunities for students to make their own materials, such as their own slide shows.

However, student-generated can mean more than just that the materials are written by those students or found by them. In keeping with our emphasis on student-centeredness, student-generated should also mean that the content flows from students' interests and needs. If students are writing texts with which they have no felt connection or they are finding texts on topics which have no appeal to them, have we really moved forward? This point is illustrated in the experience of an ESL teacher in China (Malcolm, 1996). The teacher had been teaching a Writing class that focused on different types of letters, such as letters to make appointments or to report information. The students had studied all this before and were just going through the motions, writing unconvincing letters full of careless errors. The teacher knew that something had to be done before everyone – students and teacher – collapsed from boredom. Here's what the teacher did. He read a short story to the class, and invited the class to create their own book of stories. Students enjoyed the story, and enthusiastically began writing their own, going through the writing process, caring about the quality of what they were writing. The question in students' minds changed from "What do I have to do for English?" to "What can English do for me?"

The story judged by the class to be the best was by a student who previously had been among the worst writers in the class. When the course ended, this student gave the teacher a letter of thanks (abridged below):

> Previously, my writing teachers gave me low marks. I doubted my ability. I reckoned myself as not a manager of the language. Hence, wherever I wrote, I paid little attention to it, just carried it on as a task. But you encouraged me. Self-confidence was part of my character again. So, when you asked us to write a short story, I decided to write my real experience, and it was a success, because I had become a manager of language. I am encouraged more than I can say. (p. 33)

TV soaps

Media is a very important ally for second language learners as teachers of language students must prepare the students for real or authentic listening situations with language that is, as Field (2002, p. 244) says, "the type of foreign language listening that occurs in a real-life encounter or in response to authentic material," which, he says, "is very different" from that of a text that has been graded for a language learner. TV soaps provide such examples of authentic language that is real and has not been graded for any particular level. Teachers can adjust input to whatever level they want to teach; all that the teacher has to do is to make certain to activate the students' world knowledge of the soap schemata before starting this activity. Farrell (2006) has designed the following six-stage approach to using TV soaps to encourage Learner Autonomy that teacher can adapt to their own learners' needs:

TV Soaps

- **Stage 1: Fun**
The students are asked to watch a particular TV soap and have fun. No response is required.

- **Stage 2: Names and Faces**
Students are next asked to listen only for the names of the characters on the show. They should write these and try to draw a picture of each person.

- **Stage 3: Relationships**
Students now have to establish the relationships between these individuals.

- **Stage 4: Personalities**
At this stage, the students should be taught the necessary vocabulary to describe personalities in order to write a personality description of all the characters they have identified and, also, to write about which characters they like and/or dislike.

- **Stage 5: Summary**
By this time, the students should be ready to watch for story content. They will be asked to write a summary of that day or week's show.

- **Stage 6: Fun (Again)**
The cycle comes full circle and fun returns to watching TV soaps in English.

The use of TV soaps is an excellent way to promote Learner Autonomy because it can show that TV programs in English can be accessible to students of all levels of proficiency, and that English language learning can even be fun.

Practicing vigilance

The story by Ian Malcom (Malcom, 1996) of the experience of an ESL teacher in China illustrated in the section "Bring Your Own Piece (BYOP) jigsaw" above shows how the students can come alive when given an opportunity to exercise control.

Role of teachers

When students have more explicit control over their own learning, as a true CLT approach to second language learning suggests, teachers need to be more flexible in allowing this and thus become true facilitators of learning. No longer can everything be planned to the minute in each of our classes; no longer can we (or should we) know that we'll be on Unit 4 by the fifth week of the term, no longer can we always dust off and reuse the same trusty lesson we've been using for who remembers how long. This situation adds spontaneity to teaching, but it now requires us teachers to stay on our teaching toes. But this is a good thing because now we can look for learning opportunities and teachable moments that we would not normally be open to in planned lessons because we would be focused on following the plan. Fortunately, now our second language students are available to help us with some of the preparation work that was formerly only the teachers' sole responsibility. This also shows our students that they have certain responsibilities and roles when attempting to become autonomous learners.

Role of students

Sometimes the slaves become enamored of their chains and are reluctant to accept freedom. Having teachers make all the decisions can become the accepted and expected practice. So, if the students are given more scope for self-determination, they may reject it and criticize the teachers who offer it. The opposite extreme occurs when students warmly welcome that freedom but use it for purposes other than learning. A frequent example is when students use time allotted for group discussion to talk about everything under the sun except what their groups' focus was supposed to be. We maintain however that when we give our students the freedom to discover their own learning possibilities they will lift their perceived chains of learning past and rise to these freedoms by making wise learning choices for themselves. For example, second language students may want to take part in choosing the media (see also above) in which they learn, such as learning via online or print resources, and the way in which they present their idea, e.g., doing presentations that involve songs, simulations, video, or animation. In this way, students are exposed to a broader range of possibilities when they hear about or see what their classmates are doing or have done.

Conclusion

This chapter outlined the concept of Learner Autonomy where second language students begin from a dependent position learning the second language from the teacher to independence in using the second language autonomously, or from a near total dependency on the second language teacher in the beginning of the learning process to near independence as they learn how to direct their own education. Second language students can become autonomous learners by acknowledging their preferred learning style and by monitoring their use of and exploiting their use of appropriate learning strategies. In other words, they focus on their strengths and limit their weaknesses. Of course controversies remain in this Learner Autonomy essential of the CLT paradigm such as to what extent and at what point should second language teachers intervene when students are, in our opinion, making incorrect decisions? And how much control should students have over curriculum decisions? After all, teachers are supposed to be the second language education experts and our students come to us for direction, and we are the ones with the teaching qualifications. It is good to recognize these issues while at the same time realizing that the ultimate aim of our second language students is to become proficient in the second language so that they can become fully autonomous and successful members of our.

Reflections

- What does Learner Autonomy mean to you?
- What does learner-centeredness mean to you?
- What are the differences between Learner Autonomy and learner-centeredness?
- Are you a learner-centered teacher? How do you know?
- How can teachers encourage students to learn for themselves?
- Do you think teachers should always choose learning materials for their students to study? If yes, why? If no, why not?
- What is a situation in which you could encourage your students to bring in their own materials? How can computers and the internet help students find and share materials?

- Reread the vignette at the beginning of this chapter. Do you think John is a typical language teacher or not? Explain your answer.
- Did you ever have similar reflections as John? Explain.
- What does John mean by "teach and then get out of the way"?
- Do you have a similar maxim?
- If not, what maxim or maxims would you use to explain how you interpret Learner Autonomy?

Emphasize the Social Nature of Learning

3

Vignette

A new academic year has commenced in David Rodriquez's university ESL class. David is only in his second year of language teaching, but he is a firm believer in the use of group activities, based on his own experiences as a learner and on the research and theory he read while studying for his MA TESL. Unfortunately, things aren't going as well as he had hoped. On the first day of class, David assigned students to work in groups so as to get a mix in each group based on proficiency in English and age level, as many non-traditional (older) students were taking the course. Some of the groups don't seem to be clicking so well; not much discussion takes place in these groups, their work doesn't seem to show any of the "two heads are better than one" magic promised in the research, and students have come up to David after class to complain about some of their groupmates and have asked to switch to a group with classmates they were already friends with. But David has faith that cooperative learning activities can work because they worked when he was a college student and they had worked pretty well with his ESL students last year. So, David went to the library and also talked with his more experienced colleague Melodee Metzger. Based on what he learned from his reading and from Melodee, David plans to try two things to make group work more successful in his class. First, he has decided to do some teambuilding activities in which students tell their partners about themselves. Second, when he sets up group tasks, he's going to pay more attention to creating tasks in which students really need their groupmates' help and input in order to complete the task successfully. For example, students will do the cooperative learning technique *Write-Pair-Switch* in which they first work alone to *Write*, then *Pair* with a partner and tell the partner what they wrote and why they wrote it, and finally *Switch* partners and tell their new partner what their first partner had written and the thinking behind their writing.

As discussed in the previous chapter on Learner Autonomy, this next essential element within the CLT approach to second language education emphasizes the Social Nature of Learning. As with Learner Autonomy, the Social Nature of Learning also places our second language students at the center of attention, offering them one means of taking on more rights and responsibilities in their own language learning. Furthermore, in the way that David Rodriquez has decided to implement groupwork activities in the opening vignette to this chapter, process, rather than product, is emphasized, as second language students do not just tell or show each other their answers; rather they explain to one another how they arrived at the answers (Slavin, 1995). Additionally, the Social Nature of Learning acknowledges the place of affect in second language education, highlighting the importance of positive interdependence among peers, i.e., the feeling among the members of a peer group that the group sinks or swims together, that the group is only as strong as its weakest member (Johnson & Johnson, 2009). Positive interdependence helps second language students feel support and belonging, at the same time that they are motivated to try hard to assist the group in reaching its goals. Three particular ways that second language teachers can implement this view of learning as being a social entity are,

1. To encourage second language students to learn from one another rather than solely from the teacher and the materials, such as the textbook.
2. To encourage second language students to learn from the communities in which they live and interact on a daily basis and, further, from the world beyond.
3. To encourage second language students and everyone at their educational institution to make a cooperative, rather than a competitive or individualist, stance their first option in terms of their perspective toward their fellow second language students, their teachers, and with whomever else they have contact.

Thus, this chapter outlines and discusses the Social Nature of Learning as it applies to an overall approach to CLT within second language education and suggests that second language teachers can actively implement more student–student collaboration in their classes so that the students can further develop their second language skills and abilities.

The social nature of learning

One of the basic tenets of the social nature of all learning is that we can learn from each other rather than trying to learn by ourselves. This idea can be carried over into our second language classrooms when we realize that our students can also learn from and with their peers. Whereas in the traditional approach or paradigm, the rules often were, "Eyes on your own paper," and "No talking to your neighbor," the goal in the Social Nature of Learning essential is to encourage our students to share with their peers and their teachers. Indeed, research suggests that second language students learn from and teach others all the time, especially when they are not in formal teaching settings (Breen, 2001), and more specifically within a CLT approach, as Richards and Rodgers (2001) have noted, it is actually expected that second language students will interact with their classmates in speech and writing during class activities as well as outside of class. In order for this to happen though, both second language teachers and their students need to be aware of cooperative learning skills.

Cooperative learning (also known as collaborative learning) is one of the most researched methods in all of education, with thousands of studies having been done involving a wide range of students, as to age, ethnicity, and nationality, and a wide range of subject areas, including second language. These studies suggest that cooperative learning can lead to gains of cognitive and affective variables. What should be emphasized is that it is seldom useful for teachers to just ask students to form groups and work together. Instead, preparation must take place. The literature on cooperative learning offers principles and techniques to aid in this preparation.

Many students need some preparation for group activities as they may not be accustomed to working with classmates on academic tasks. Instead, they may have mostly experienced teacher-fronted instruction. To prepare students to cooperate, second language teachers often include explicit instruction in cooperative skills. The teaching of cooperative skills is a cooperative learning principle. Examples of these cooperative skills include praising others, asking for help, and giving and receiving suggestions (Gillies, 2007). These cooperative skills are also vital second language skills; skills that will serve our second language students well in their future academic careers and in other aspects of their lives where they collaborate with others.

Johnson and Johnson (1999) explain a useful six-step procedure for facilitating students' regular use of cooperative skills that can be used in second language classrooms:

1. Students understand why a particular skill is important.
2. Students know the words, phrases, gestures, etc. typical of use of that one skill.
3. Students practice the skill in isolation, e.g., they do a game or role play that features the skill.
4. Students use the skill during a cooperative learning activity involving regular course content.
5. Students monitor their use of the skills and discuss their findings.
6. The skill is emphasized in an ongoing way, rather than just once.

Another means second language teachers have of promoting collaboration in their classrooms is to foster an overall atmosphere in which cooperation acts not just as a methodology for second language learning, but also a topic in itself for learning, and as a value embraced in all learning activities (Jacobs, Power, and Loh, 2002). Examples of cooperation as a topic for learning would be second language students writing compositions about the times that they (or people whom they interview if this can be incorporated into the course) have collaborated with others. To establish cooperation as a value, the class as a group can look at what processes in the school, such as norm-referenced evaluation and in society, such as contests with only one winner, promote competition as a value. It should be noted that the aim is not to eliminate competition or individual work; the aim is to achieve a better balance.

One way to encourage students to think in terms of cooperating with others, in particular others outside the class involves service learning projects (Roehlkepartain, 2009; National Service Learning Clearing House, 2009 http://servicelearning.org). Service learning is the combination of service to others with learning related to students' course curriculum. Learning could be added to the same experience in several ways:

- Investigation. Students could, work in pairs to study the eating habits of other students. Pairs, where possible would be formed by people with different first language backgrounds (or different L1s); if the entire class has a common L1, students could decide to devote a percentage of the time to speaking the second language (or L2) and could study vocabulary they would need in that discussion.
- Planning. Before beginning their service learning actions, students could discuss what would be a good project to do toward improving people's eating habits.
- Implementing. Students could prepare talks, posters, flyers to encourage others to eat more wisely and then could arrange to do the talks and disseminate the materials they had prepared.

These service learning activities provide opportunities for students to learn together for a purpose other than to get a high score on an exam, although the learning that takes place might lead to higher exam scores. An example of a service learning project done by second language students is documented by Wilhelm (2006), whose university ESL students in Illinois did presentations on U. S. culture for preschool students.

Classroom implications

Group work

The most common way that teachers can implement this view of learning as a social activity is by the use of cooperative learning activities in their second language classes. As noted above, cooperative learning offers second language teachers many ideas for how they can go beyond merely asking students to work together in pairs or groups. Different techniques will be appropriate with different learning goals and will match with different views of teaching;

furthermore, techniques can be adapted to fit particular learning situations. We now outline and discuss two group techniques: *Snowball* and *Building Community*.

Snowball

Snowball (adapted from Kearney, 1993) is actually two techniques in one: *Forward Snowball* and *Reverse Snowball*. *Forward Snowball* involves students in working together to *generate* ideas, and in *Reverse Snowball*, students choose from among the ideas their group has *generated*. *Forward Snowball* is used for brainstorming and highlights the benefit of heterogeneity because it is good for gathering as many ideas or as much information as possible.

- Step 1 – Each group member works alone to list ideas or information.
- Step 2 – Pairs explain their lists to each other and then make a combined list. Duplications are eliminated.
- Step 3 – Pair One and Pair Two get together and make a combined list. Duplications are eliminated.

Forward Snowball is also useful for teambuilding (creating bonds among group members) because it provides dramatic proof that two (or more) heads really are better than one. Within second language teaching such as an English as a second language (ESL) class, *Forward Snowball* can be used as follows: The teacher writes a word on the board, such as "important." Students do *Forward Snowball* to see how many words they can generate using the letters of "important." Perhaps they can use various aids, such as electronic dictionaries and websites, to find more words.

In *Forward Snowball*, the group's list gets bigger and bigger, however, in *Reverse Snowball*, it gets smaller. Thus, this technique builds analysis and evaluation skills as in the following steps:

- Step 1 – Each group member works alone to list ideas or information.
- Step 2 – Pairs explain their lists to each other and then make a list of only those items that appear on both lists or only those that they think are the best.
- Step 3 – Two pairs repeat the same process.

Reverse Snowball could work as follows: Each group member lists four examples of good writing in a particular text. By Step 3 of *Reverse Snowball*, they try to agree on the best example of good writing in the text and prepare to explain their choice.

Snowball is a useful cooperative learning technique because each member works alone first and then presents to the group, thus students are discouraged from either doing nothing or, the opposite, attempting to dominate the group. The group has a common goal, e.g., in *Forward Snowball*, their goal is to make a long list, and each group member contributes to that goal. Also, the group has a single product and this encourages them to work together.

Building community

Important factors in successful collaboration are feelings of caring, trust, and safety. Students are more likely to ask for help, take risks, and share with others in an atmosphere in which people care about, respect, and protect one another. At the same time that we are part of a community, we also maintain our individual identities. Creating such an atmosphere takes time and skilled effort. We present the following ideas for promoting this community spirit in second language classrooms.

- *Discussing group functioning.* One way to foster collaborative skills (one of the cooperative learning principles mentioned above) is for individual groups and the class as a whole to discuss how groups are functioning (Gibbs, 2006). For instance, a group that has been working together fairly well can share with the rest of the class their ideas about what helped them work well together. Other topics for group and class discussion are what groups can do to work better in the future and how students can apply what they have learned about groups in the classroom to groups they are in outside the classroom.
- *Electronic cooperation.* Information technology offers a wide and growing array of opportunities for students to work together. For instance, chat software provides for synchronous (at the same time) interaction among students. E-groups involve asynchronous (at different times) interaction. These electronic forums can be open only to course members. Blogs are yet another form of electronic communication. Then, of course, there is old-fashioned email. For example, students can mail their work to each other, give each other feedback, using such features as Track Changes and Comments in MS Word, and then send the work back to the original author. Yet another software, Etherpad allows two people on different computers to simultaneously type on the same document (www.etherpad.com).
- *Groups helping other groups.* When cooperative learning is used successfully, groups believe that their task is not completed until,

    a. everyone in the *group* understands the concepts being taught and has improved their skills. For instance, if a group has finished answering the problems in a grammar textbook, they are not finished until everyone in the group, working alone, could do all the problems and explain how they arrived at their answers;

b. everyone in the *class* understands the concepts being taught and has improved their skills. Thus, a group is not done just because it has finished their task. Instead, all the group members look around the room to see if other groups might be able to benefit from their assistance. In this way, the feeling of positive inter-dependence, i.e., "all for one, one for all," extends beyond the small classroom group to encompass the entire class.

Cooperative learning can take place in many different places and with many different types of people. Here are some examples:

- *Cross-age tutoring* (from Fisher, 2001). In cross-age tutoring, older second language students work with younger students. For instance, upper elementary school Spanish as a second language students can read aloud to lower elementary school students and help the younger Spanish as a Second Language students with their writing. The older students provide positive models to the younger ones, and the older ones build confidence and skills in the process. Ideally, such tutoring programs involve even lower-proficiency older students, as the experience can provide these lower-proficiency students a boost to their motivation and self-esteem.
- *Out-of-class academic collaboration*. Bloom (1984) states that peer interaction out-side the classroom – not just inside the classroom – can also be crucial to academic success. Such out-of-class academic collaboration (OCAC) can be organized in at least three ways.

  o Institutionally-sponsored OCAC, e.g., peer tutoring programs established by institutions where students who are more proficient in English are chosen by the institution (and sometimes paid or otherwise rewarded) to tutor students weak in that subject. These programs may be sponsored by the institution where students are studying, or by other organizations, such as religious or ethnic organizations.
  o Teacher-initiated OCAC, e.g., a teacher assigns students to work together on an ESL homework assignment. Project work is another area in which teachers often organize students to work together outside of class.
  o Student-initiated OCAC, e.g., a group of students meet together on their own to study for an examination or to complete an ESL assignment.

Project work

Another way second language students can be encouraged to work collabora-tively together is by engaging in project work (Beckett & Miller, 2006). Projects, such as those involving service learning, offer students an opportu-nity to break down the artificial walls that often separate them from the wider world (Freire, 1970). Projects can take many forms and can last anywhere from

30 minutes to several months. One cooperative learning method for facilitating longer-term projects is Group Investigation (Tan, Sharan, & Lee, 2006). Here, the class functions as a group of groups, with the class choosing an overall theme, such as careers, and each group deciding to study one career, such as tennis instructor, or one aspect of careers, such as how to be promoted or achieve a salary increase. Within each group, members make a plan, divide up the work, report back to and consult each other frequently, and put together a report to present to the other groups. Group activities can also play a role in the groups' presentation. Rather than each group, one at a time, coming to the front to present, while their classmates sit motionless soaking in the presentation, group activities can be used here as well. For example, the presenters can give their audience issues to discuss with a partner, or the audience members can interview each other. Group Investigation is very similar to what is perhaps now a better-known method, Problem-based Learning (Hmelo-Silver & Barrows, 2006).

Grading group/project work

One important question we should consider at this stage is, should group members all receive the same grade? If students have worked together on a project or some other task, giving everyone in the group the same grade makes sense for several reasons:

- Many times in life, groups succeed or fail together. For instance, if people are working together to support or oppose a ballot initiative, they all win or lose, regardless of how much each contributed to the effort.
- Positive interdependence may increase when students all receive the same grade. Thus, students may be more willing to ask for and give each other help.
- Determining how much each student contributed to their group can be very difficult.

At the same time, a number of good reasons can be given for why group members should each receive a separate grade such as,

- People looking at students' grade, such as university admissions officers, may have difficulty interpreting what a group grade says about an individual student's ability and work.
- The same student could get a different grade depending on their groupmates. With higher achieving and more motivated groupmates, a higher grade would be likely.

- Students may be demotivated if they feel their grade doesn't clearly reflect what they themselves have contributed.

A third option when grades are used to accompany group activities lies in using a combination of individual and group grading. Consequently, second language teachers have a very important role to play when setting up cooperative learning activities in their classes and these roles along with student roles, will be outlined in the following sections.

In addition to the above activities we suggest several ways by which the materials teachers use to accomplish these activities can promote collaboration among second language students. These include the following:

- The materials or teachers' guides that accompany them can give specific suggestions for which activities to do via collaboration among students and how such collaboration should be organized.
- Students and teachers can use their own knowledge and experience to decide these issues.
- Rather than relying on existing materials, students can rely on one another as well as others in the school and beyond to locate learning materials and can develop their materials for themselves and others. An example of students developing their own materials is when students do research, e.g., by interviewing classmates, family members, and others, write a report on their findings, and disseminate their report.

Practicing vigilance

This story comes from the fictional tales of Nassredin, a character from Turkey, known for being sly at times. In this story, Nassredin found a job as a teacher, but he did his best to teach as little as possible.

Nassredin began the first day of school by asking students, "Do you know what I will be teaching you?" When the students replied that they did not know, "Since you do not even know what I will be teaching, there is no point in my even trying to teach," and he immediately left the classroom and adjourned to his favorite cafe.

On the second day of school, Nassredin repeated his question. The eager students were prepared this time. Therefore, they responded with an enthusiastic "Yes." However, Nassredin was ready too, and quickly replied, "Oh, as you already know what I plan to teach, it would be a waste of everyone's time for me to teach you," and again, he immediately left the class. In just a few minutes, he was making himself comfortable with a potent cup of espresso.

The third day, the students had a plan to outsmart their sly and reluctant teacher. When he asked the students if they knew what he was there to teach, half of the expectant learners said "Yes," while the other half replied, "No." However, Nassredin, without missing a beat, responded with his own misguided version of cooperative learning, "Oh good," he said while heading out the door. "In that case, those of you who know, please teach those of you who don't know."

Role of teachers

When teachers use a Social Nature of Learning focus within a CLT approach to second language education they will usually,

- Be observers, noticing such phenomena as how well students are working together, their understanding of the material, and the process by which they are going about their work.
- Participate in work similar to what students are doing, either alone or as a group member. For instance, if students are doing science projects, they can join a group or be doing a project of their own, perhaps with people outside a school, e.g., a local environmental organization.
- Give students space to try to learn on their own. The way that most teachers use group activities is to first give some teacher input and then have a group activity in which students use in some way what the teacher has taught. But what if, instead, students had reached the point of group autonomy in which they could reduce the time needed for teacher input or move it to a later part of the lesson? In other words, students would be reaching a stage in which they don't always need the teacher to predigest everything for them – even materials written especially for students.

Role of students

Students play a wide range of roles as they interact with peers and others. Within a group, possible roles include (Jacobs, Power, & Loh, 2002) the following:

- *Facilitator* (also called Coach) – keeps the group on task and checks that everyone knows what the instructions are
- *Time Keeper* – keeps track of the time limits
- *Checker* – checks to see that all group members have understood
- *Encourager* (also called Cheerleader) – encourages everyone to participate and leads the celebration of success

- *Recorder* – keeps notes on what the group has discussed – these can be in normal note form or in the shape of a graphic organizer, such as word webs or mind maps
- *Reporter* – reports the group's work to other groups or the whole class
- *Materials Manager* – makes sure the group has the materials it needs and that these are properly taken care of
- *Questioner* – asks questions to prompt the group to go more deeply and broadly into their task
- *Summarizer* – highlights the main things the group has discussed, keeps track of the group's progress
- *Paraphraser* – restates what the previous speaker said to check comprehension
- *Praiser* – compliments groupmates for their ideas and their role in the group
- *Elaborator* – connects the group's ideas to other things they have studied or to out-of-school contexts
- *Safety Monitor* – helps to see that safety procedures are followed when groups use potentially dangerous equipment
- *Conflict Creator* – plays the role of devil's advocate bringing out opposing points of view and other possibilities, as well as unearthing the conflicting ideas that are already in the group but that are being unexpressed or ignored
- *Sound Hound* – makes sure the noise level does not go too high
- *Observer* – notes how the group is working together and reports this back to the group.

These roles rotate so that students have opportunities to try on different responsibilities for group success.

Conclusion

To understand and promote learning, we look not only at individuals but also at the people who make up their world and the connections among them. These people include not only teachers, but also peers, and others in the community. This chapter has suggested that cooperation is valued over competing or working alone, although there is still a place for competition and individual work. When students collaborate they all play leadership roles. The chapter suggests that we focus greater attention on the Social Nature of Learning in our second language classes rather than on students as separate, decontextualized individuals because ultimately this will make second language learning more accessible and more enjoyable for our students.

Reflection

- Review the opening story of this chapter and ask yourself why group work may fail in many second language classes?
- What do you think of David's ideas on implementing group work in his classes?
- Have you ever used group work in your classes? If yes, how did you set these groups up and how did you evaluate their level of success?
- If no, how do you think you would go about implementing group work in your class?
- What can you do as a second language teacher to ensure all members of the group participate and cooperate?
- How do you or would you grade group work? What would be your rationale for such grading?
- What do you think is the greatest obstacle to using group work successfully in your classes? How would you overcome this?
- What would you do if one student said that he or she does not like group work and anyway it is not part of his or her cultural background?
- What would you do if one student said that he or she paid you, the teacher, to teach and not his or her classmates and that he or she feels cheated with this method of learning?
- What do you think are the roles of both teachers and students within group work?

4 Develop Curricular Integration

Vignette

Jane Smith is a master at integrating the curriculum in her fourth grade ESL classroom. She instinctively knows how to help students see and make connections between the English language/Language arts and among other things they are studying in their classes. Jane Smith makes sure that her students realize that almost all science, math, and social studies lessons are connected in some way to Language arts. For instance, as part of a science unit on the water cycle, Jane pointed out to her students that they can apply their knowledge and understanding of the water cycle to write a creative monologue in English about the life cycle of a water droplet, thus practicing all they learned from Jane about the writing process in English. Before the writing assignment, which emphasized using descriptive detail, the students were asked to complete a pre-writing activity in which they visited seven stations representing each of the places water is found: rivers, oceans, plants, reservoirs, ground water, soil, and lakes, with particular emphasis on local instance. This helps students see the relevance of the lesson to their own lives. Equipped with the language and content knowledge gained and remembered from this pre-writing activity, students wrote initial drafts. Then, in their groups of four, they took turns sitting in the author's chair and reading their stories to their groupmates who listened and offered comments and compliments. In this way, the various language skills are integrated, as first students write, then they read and speak, while groupmates listen. One of Jane's students, Pamela, a particularly dramatic student, received a great deal of positive feedback from her peers on the first draft of her story, both due to her expressive reading and the humorous details she incorporated into her narrative. Pamela's group broke into laughter and applause when she read the following in a high, squeaky voice, "I was swallowed by a big salamander, and he peed me out as a big, yellow puddle!" Groupmates then tried to follow Pamela's example when they rewrote their own drafts. Here, the academic (science and language arts) is linked with the social and emotional, as groupmates listen and respond to each other's efforts. Jane is convinced that, in her teaching, she must continue to point out how each subject area is linked to other subjects and to the world beyond the school, and how knowledge and skills of the English language, her students' second language, are necessary for success.

Integrated curriculum can be defined in a variety of ways. For our purposes, we focus on linking language with other curricular areas, on linking the various language skills, on linking the academic with the social and emotional aspects of students' lives, on linking different ways of learning, and on linking classroom activities to the wider world. Sometimes these links are small connections within a single lesson, and at other times, the links involve larger concepts that unify a course of study. Many opportunities to make connections between various parts of the curriculum present themselves, and it is the responsibility of teachers and administrators to recognize and reinforce these opportunities.

Many of the ideas advocated in this book are supported by the findings of recent research on how the brain works. Integrated Curriculum is one example. Brain research tells us that our minds are constantly looking for connections (Jensen, 2008). Integrated Curriculum guides students to find and create the many connections that exist to be explored.

A key link between Curricular Integration in education generally, and the CLT paradigm shift in second language education, lies in the concept of going from whole to part rather than from part to whole. For instance, under the traditional education model, students study a given historical period, e.g., the 19th century, in an atomistic way. In history class, they study key events, people and movements. In science class, in another year or semester, they discuss notable scientific discoveries from the 19th century. In first or second language class, in yet another year or semester, they read literature from the period. Thus, students miss valuable opportunities for understanding context.

In second language class, students might read about one topic, listen to conversations about a different topic, and write about a third topic, or they might read or listen to a text in one text type and write a text in a different text type. Thus, not only are connections missing between language class and the other subjects the students might be studying, or the careers they might be pursuing or planning to pursue, but connections are not even made across different aspects of the language curriculum. Jane Smith, the fourth grade ESL teacher, attempted to show her students how different subjects are linked and then gave them practical examples of how this worked while also showing them the importance of mastery of English language skills so that they can be successful in all their subject areas. This chapter outlines and discusses the concept of integrated curriculum and shows from a practical perspective how second language teachers can utilize this concept to ensure their students are studying within a CLT approach to language learning.

Curricular integration

Curricular Integration serves to overcome the phenomenon in which students study one subject in one period, close their textbook and go to another class, open another textbook and study another subject. When various subject areas are taught jointly, learners have more opportunities to see the links between subject areas. By appreciating these links, students develop a stronger grasp of subject matter, a deeper purpose for learning and a greater ability to analyze situations in a holistic manner (Brinton, Snow, & Wesche, 1989). Curricular Integration is just one of the many aspects of the CLT paradigm that overlaps with a more recent trend in second language education, the standards movement.

The concept of language across the curriculum offers one route for implementing a Curricular Integration (Chamot & O'Malley, 1994). The idea is that language competence is necessary for learning in all subject areas. For instance, students cannot understand their textbooks if they have weak reading skills; they cannot do tasks if they have weak speaking and writing skills. As students develop their language skills, they simultaneously deepen their grasp of content matter. For example, asking students to write, even in mathematics class, about what they understand, what they are unclear about and how they can apply what they have learned offers a powerful means of deepening students' competence in a subject area.

In second language education, another means of implementing Curricular Integration is content-based instruction (Crandall, 1987; Shrum & Glisan, 2000). In content-based instruction, rather than lessons focusing mainly on the second language, the second language becomes the vehicle for learning about content that connects to students' needs and/or interests. As Wilga Rivers (1976, p. 96), an authority on second language education since the 1960s, has written, "As language teachers we are the most fortunate of teachers – all subjects are ours. Whatever [the students] want to communicate about, whatever they want to read about, is our subject matter." Therefore, we have the flexibility to work with students to craft curriculum.

Project work is yet another method of implementing Curricular Integration, in that projects are often multidisciplinary (Ribe & Vidal, 1993). For example, an environmental project, e.g., on water pollution, could involve scientific knowledge about how to analyze water samples, mathematics knowledge to do calculations based on the sample, social studies knowledge about the role of governmental, private, and civic sectors in cleaning up water pollution and language knowledge to write letters and prepare presentations based on the project's findings. This example of using projects as a tool for integration across content areas also exemplifies integrating instruction with students' lives beyond the classroom, as an adequate supply of clean water matters to everyone. One concept related to this integration of education and life is termed critical pedagogy. Critical pedagogy encourages a view of learning as a process in which students actively take part in transforming themselves and their world, rather than learning being a process in which students passively take part in the transmission of information from their teachers and textbooks to themselves (Crookes & Lehner, 1998; Vandrick, 1999).

Language for Specific Purposes (LSP) (Robinson, 1980) provides an additional path toward Curricular Integration. For example, a group of hotel employees studying Japanese might focus on the Japanese they need in their work. Thus, the conversations they listen to and practice might involve exchanges between hotel guests and staff, and the material they read might include hotel brochures and other travel industry literature. Their language learning clearly integrates with their occupational needs.

Classroom implications

Here are more ways to implement various aspects of Curricular Integration.

- *Parallel topics* – instruction in several subjects is organized around a common topic such as Mexico. Students may study the history of Mexico in Social Studies, read literature from Mexico in language arts, and create Mexican folk arts in art class. Although the topic is parallel in each of the subjects, instruction does not emphasize making connections between disciplines.
- *Interdisciplinary Instruction* – instruction is organized to help students more readily find the connections between disciplines. Students might study the concept of proportion in math and art and the concept of fractions in math and music. The emphasis is on understanding a concept from the perspective of more than one discipline.
- *Immersion experiences* – learning is organized to more closely resemble life. Within this real-life context, students find meaning. Students might organize a service project to provide coats for children in need. Students learn skills and concepts from multiple disciplines within the context of real-life problems.

The following continuum (Figure 4.1) illustrates increasing levels of integration.

There are varied approaches to creating more integrated settings for learning, many of which are discussed later in the chapter. In general, quality integrated instruction is organized to include materials from a *variety of resources, interdisciplinary investigation,* and *higher-level thinking.*

Separate Disciplines	Parallel Topics	Interdisciplinary Instruction	Immersion Experiences

Figure 4.1 Increasing levels of integration

Variety of resources

The possibilities for curriculum integration are endless, ranging from small connections within a single lesson to more lengthy and complex units of study. There are a variety of rich, multi-disciplinary resources that can enrich a lesson or unit. They may be used to teach concepts, motivate and engage students, promote critical thinking through experiences, or represent learning in multiple forms. The following list suggests some of the more common strategies.

Teach a concept with children's literature, music, art, or other resources

- A language arts teacher uses the book "Listen to the Rain" to help middle school students understand the concept of onomatopoeia.
- A science teacher uses stringed instruments to help students study the physics of sound production.

Promote higher-level reasoning through experiences

- Students participate in Báfa báfa, a cross-cultural contact simulation, to better understand elements of trade and cultural diffusion.
- Students participate in the Project Wild activity, "How Many Bears Can Live in this Forest?" Students "walk into the forest" as bears with different characteristics (injured young male, female blinded by porcupine quills, and mother bear with cubs), gather food cards and then return to their dens.
- During a science unit students assume the role of crickets, birds, or hawks. They simulate the dynamics in the food chain through a game of tag.

All of the previously mentioned examples focus on incorporating rich resources and interdisciplinary activities within more traditional lessons. Please note also the wide range of intelligences brought to bear on the topics (for more on Multiple Intelligences, please see the chapter on Diversity). To expand connective thinking, there are a variety of more structured models that help teachers think about organizing curriculum in an integrated fashion.

Interdisciplinary units

In this model, a topic, theme/concept or piece of literature usually serves as the organizing framework for a collection of lessons over an expanded period, usually two to four weeks. The unit examines the topic/theme from the perspective of two or more disciplines and may contain many of the types of activities listed previously. Varied resources from multiple disciplines are then sequenced to expand students' understandings. The degree of integration varies by unit, ranging from incorporation of activities around a topic such as China, to complex units organizing study around a central theme such as Interdependence.

Topical unit example

In the simplest form, a study of the topic China would include varied activities. These might include reading a piece of Chinese literature, working with tangrams, creating Chinese paper cuts, sampling food, map studies, and noting cultural treasures such as the Great Wall and the terra cotta warrior figures. Upon unit completion, students will know many new things about China but not necessarily how they are interconnected.

Thematic or conceptual unit example

In a thematic unit, the teacher may use the same activities as those in a topical unit but with the added lens of the theme to guide students in finding connections. Let's return to the example of China. We can give a conceptual focus to the unit on China by identifying a theme such as interdependence, adaptation, change and continuity, or conflict. Selecting interdependence as the theme shifts the way China is studied while guiding students toward recognizing that examples of interdependence are found in all time periods across the world. Thus, sampling Chinese food includes an examination of how peoples' diets depend upon the food resources produced in a region. In the north, wheat-based products are common. In southern China, the climate supports growing rice and its inclusion as a dietary staple. Since arable and grazing lands are at a premium, pork products (hogs require very little pen space) and ocean/river products (fish, eel, squid) become the meat staples. Diets depend upon the available resources.

The theme of interdependence shapes a focus for studying about the Great Wall of China. The original series of many walls were built to protect the territories of different rulers from their warring neighbors. The first emperor of China united the northern ends of these walls to protect the people from invading Mongols from the north. Thus, the separate kingdoms came to depend upon each other to protect themselves from invaders. Each lesson on an aspect of Chinese life adds a layer to understanding how pervasive interdependence is.

It is important to remember that a good theme is a broad concept that crosses the disciplines. Since there are many themes, the first task is for the teacher to select a theme to use in exploring a topic. The following questions aid in identifying a theme:

- Does it apply to different disciplines?
- Can it be applied to different times and places?
- Does it reveal similarities and contrasts?
- Does it fascinate?

For example, the concept of interdependence is a lens for finding patterns in life. The following list shows how different disciplines might address the theme of interdependence.

- Social studies

  o Family members
  o Trade
  o Political systems

- Science

  o Food chain
  o Ecological systems
  o Water cycle
  o Acid rain

- Mathematics

  o Operations
  o Balancing equations

- Language arts/ESL

  o Context in reading/writing
  o Story lines

- Music

  o Chorus/orchestra
  o Musical compositions

Once you start looking for examples of interdependence, you begin to realize that the possibilities are endless. Thus, interdisciplinary instruction makes learning fun and meaningful as follows: The integrative nature of interdisciplinary units encourages students to "see" the interconnectedness of the world around them. This linking renders the world more relevant by connecting content, self, and community. Understanding the links generates excitement and fuels the desire to learn more.

Integrative studies

We can take a thematic unit to a higher level by adding the dimension of questioning found in the integrative studies model. The integrative studies model (Davies, 2005) is adapted from an American Studies approach to studying culture. This model uses themes, resources organized around a theme, and questions to make sense of a complex world. A theme or pattern acts as the vehicle for organization. Students are presented with a variety of resources around a theme and examine the development over time of interrelationships between data. This process promotes a deeper understanding of the theme and recognition that it is a pervasive part of life. Students discover interrelationships through time by examining data from different disciplines. This varied information might include excerpts from speeches or diaries, photographs, maps, music, poems, literature, works of art, or other primary and secondary resources. In structuring the unit, the challenge is to locate varied resources representing different ways of examining the theme. Access to web-based resources makes the task of locating materials easier. This is similar to the strategies for teaching concepts with a rich variety of resources. However, the balance provided by studying a concept from multiple disciplines and the added dimension of questioning bring depth of understanding.

Theme selected and materials assembled, the teacher uses a four-tier questioning strategy to assist students in identifying interconnections:

1. *Understand the artifact*. These questions assure that the specific artifact is understood. The questions focus on knowledge and comprehension. For example, what does the poem mean?
2. *Explore the inter-relatedness of artifacts*. Ask questions that examine the interrelatedness of artifacts and connect the data to students' prior experiences. Analysis forms the crux of this level of questioning. For example, have you ever experienced feelings similar to those expressed in the poem? Or how are the events in the poem similar/different to those identified in the timeline?
3. *Explore how data might be expressed through other perceptual modes*. Guide students in expressing data through a different mode of perception. This requires mental flexibility, a key component of creative production. For example, translate the events of the timeline into a poem.
4. *Examine the relationship of chronology to the various artifacts*. Could such a poem have been written fifty years ago? Why or why not? This stage incorporates critical and analytical thinking.

Example of Integrative Studies Model

In order to understand freedom quests as a human condition, students study several examples of quests from different eras and cultures. For example, they might examine data representing how searches for freedom influenced Chief Joseph of the Nez Perce, Harriet Tubman, Martin Luther King, Jr., Mahatma Gandhi, and so on. This allows for comparisons between quests which guide connection finding. An excerpt from an exploration of the theme, *Quests for Freedom*, illustrates this model. Sample activities from a study of Chief Joseph's quest follow.

Procedures:

1. Read Chief Joseph's quotations. What did they reveal about Nez Perce beliefs? How did these beliefs differ from those of white settlers? Was conflict inevitable between the white settlers and the Nez Perce? Explain.

   CHIEF JOSEPH'S QUOTATIONS
   The earth is the mother of all people, and all people should have equal rights upon it. The earth and myself are of one mind. The measure of the land and the measure of our bodies are the same. . . . I never said the land was mine to do with as I chose. The one who has the right to dispose of it is the one who has created it. I claim the right to live on my land and accord you the privilege to live on yours (Gidley, 1981).

2. "Play the song, Earth is Our Mother" (Gass, 1986, cited in Davies, 2000) or another selection of native American music. Direct students to rhythmically walk to the music. What does the song reveal about the Indians' relationship to the earth? Would Chief Joseph agree with the song's lyrics? Using the content of the song and the quotations, write a speech that Chief Joseph delivers to white settlers expressing his people's beliefs about the land. Does this song reflect the beliefs of American Indians today?

3. Distribute a chronology of Chief Joseph. Direct students to identify all examples of culture contact between whites and the Nez Perce. For each contact, discuss if it was a positive, negative, or neutral experience from the perspectives of the whites and the Indians. How might the world views expressed in the song and Chief Joseph's quotations help account for these interactions? Describe the changing nature of these interactions over time. What factors account for this? Write a song or poem that reflects these changing interactions from the perspective of a Nez Perce or a white settler. Create a timeline that shows these events and those influencing Harriet Tubman's life (pre-Civil War through the turn of the century). Chief Joseph and Harriet Tubman were contemporaries. Were they influenced by the same events? Why or why not? How were their experiences similar? Different?

Community connections

We can extend the concept of the integrated unit approach even further by organizing study outside the school doors. Field trips, service learning projects, and immersion experiences provide examples of connecting to the wider community.

Field trips

Many opportunities for field trips abound in the classroom and often curricular connections focus around these experiences. For instance, students that attended a musical performance of the "Voice of the Whale" also went to the local aquarium to study marine life, and explored the beach. Each of these experiences connected nicely with their science curriculum on ecosystems, the social studies focus on human interaction with the environment, and provided a variety of opportunities for reading and writing.

Service projects

Social Studies includes a focus on service learning to help students understand themselves as citizens within a larger community. The very nature of service learning presents itself as an opportunity for organizing curriculum around a purpose or project to help students see connections to real life. For instance, ESL students in a grade class can choose to restore the turtle pond that stood in the courtyard garden of their elementary school. The students can sell carnations at Valentine's Day to raise money for the project, research the ecosystem of the pond, estimate costs for materials and supplies, and write an article in the school newspaper about the project. This way they get exposure to all aspects of school, and community life while developing all skills in English.

Immersion experiences

Middle school students study some issue in history that focuses on continuity and change. In small groups, the students select topics of interest relating to their issue that includes information about education, women's roles, home crafts, and religion from that period of time. They research their topics using library, internet, and community resources. From the community a number of individuals assist in the research. For example, those researching food can get help from a local chef so he or she can help them cook the pre-planned meals over an open fire and a local fisherman can help them attempt to catch fish at a nearby pond, just as has happened during that period in history. After a day, students return to school for a debriefing. They compare life now and then and discuss factors contributing to these changes.

Integrating skills

One of the meanings of Integrated Curriculum involves linking the various language skills. Most teachers think of four skills: reading, writing, speaking (including) pronunciation, and listening. It is not uncommon for ESL programs to offer separate courses in each of these skills. Sometimes grammar is included as a separate skill and a separate course. These skills can easily be integrated. For example, group discussions can accompany reading. Of course, once students are discussing what they have read, speaking and listening have been combined with reading. Writing is easily added as well, for example, when students are asked to write about how they can use what they have learned from what they have read. Grammar could certainly come in along with the writing and speaking, and students can notice features of what they are listening to and reading (Cross, 2002).

Here is a sample reading lesson that integrates reading, writing, listening, and speaking.

> Students are doing Extensive Reading (for more on this method, see the chapter of Learner Autonomy). After each has finished a book, they meet in a group of two to tell each other about what they have read. First, students write a brief summary of their book to help them prepare to share about it with their partner. The partners ask each other questions. (The teacher has led the class to develop these questions – which will vary depending on the type of book – and to develop ways to answer them). Then, two groups of two combine to share about their books, but this time, each student tells about the book that their partner read. One goal here is that students will provide each other with ideas for good books to read next.

Integrating the academic with the social and emotional

Nowadays, we see an increased emphasis on test scores. This encourages educators to focus only on academics and to neglect the social and emotional aspects of education. Such a focus is a mistake for at least two reasons. First, by involving the social and emotional side of students, we attempt to foster an environment that boosts learners' liking for self and others, helps them develop cooperative skills and the attitudes necessary for employing such skills, increases positive behaviors, leads to more student–student and student–teacher interaction, and decreases drug use, truancy, bullying, and violent behaviors (Collaborative for Academic, Social, and Emotional Learning, 2008).

Second, if we emphasize only students' cognitive development, we are neglecting important areas of what empowers students to enjoy a successful, useful life. (Goleman, 2005)

Practicing vigilance

Read the following stories and see how teachers must be aware of how far they want to connect their classroom to the real world in the first story (*Too Real Realia*) and in the second story (*What's in a Name*) how focusing on meaning doesn't mean forgetting to teach form; it means teaching form in the context of meaning.

Too real realia

A well-meaning teacher in India believed that use of the L1 should be avoided and that potentially difficult vocabulary should be taught, to the extent possible, by way of realia. One day, he was planning to teach some of the terms for the parts of a cow's body, such as horns and tail. Thus, the logical thing to do seemed to be to bring a cow into the classroom.

This the teacher did. The lesson might have gone alright had not an officer from the local school district chosen that very day and that very class for a surprise lesson observation. The classroom was rather crowded, leaving the only place for the inspector up in front with the cow. As the teacher had aptly chosen a cow with large horns, the better to teach this vocabulary item, the inspector decided to seat himself at the other end of the cow.

This decision also had its drawbacks, as the cow felt the call of nature, and the poor inspector, who had entered the room dressed in a spotless white uniform, suddenly had his favorite uniform decorated in various shades and shapes of brown.

Needless to say, the inspector was furious and wanted to demote the teacher. However, after the teacher explained that he had only been following the guidance of his university professors, the inspector decided to let him go with just a warning, as long as he promised to forget all that the idiots at the university had taught him (Story by B. R. Sundara Rajan).

What's in a name

An ESL teacher in Bahrain was using a Study Skills book written by Richard Yorkey. (It is important to know that the first syllable receives the stress in this author's last name.) At the end of class one day, the teacher asked his students to, "Remember to bring Yorkey to the next lesson."

When the next lesson came, students were asked to take out their books, which they all did, except for one student who had nothing on her desk other than a pencil and a single key. The teacher asked, "Did you forget your Study Skills book today?" "No," the student replied. I thought you said, "Bring your key."

Here was a teachable moment, an opportunity to focus on form, in this case how English distributes stress. This is what the teacher did, in a short, simple way, before returning to the Study Skills lesson.

Role of teachers

Sometimes the teacher is more actively involved in leading student learning and at other times acts more as a facilitator, depending on the particular activity or depth of integration. If you are going to teach students connective reasoning, the teacher must model the process and look for opportunities to question students that guide their thinking to understand concepts. The teacher helps orchestrate the collection of resources and organizing experiences that will provide optimal opportunities for learning as well as providing a structure for organizing and making sense of learning.

Role of students

Learning is actively constructing meaning with focus on metacognitive skills and connective reasoning. Thus, active involvement becomes a critical learner role. The integrated curriculum offers many opportunities for engagement including making choices about areas of study, monitoring one's thinking, and experiencing topics/concepts from multi-sensory and multi-disciplinary perspectives.

Conclusion

Integrated curriculum holds great potential for deep learning in the classroom. It helps students to see connections between disciplines, to their own prior knowledge, and to real-world contexts. Integrated curriculum takes many forms, but generally it includes the use of a variety of resources, an interdisciplinary approach, and an emphasis on higher-level thinking. Although any attempt to help students see connections is worthwhile, some forms of integration are more complex and promote deeper levels of understanding. Discovering the inter-relatedness of all life is truly the challenge and reward of learning. Like the roots of a tree, we seek connections to better understand and sustain life.

Reflections

- What is your understanding of integrated curriculum?
- Have you ever tried to show your ESL students how skills in English are used throughout their studies in school?
- If yes, how did you go about this and were you successful?
- If no, how do you think you would go about this?
- What kind of Field Trips would be suitable for ESL students?
- Have you ever taken your students on a Field Trip? If yes, how did you set it up and where did you go?
- What do you think would be a good Field Trip for ESL Elementary school students and why?
- What do you think would be a good Field Trip for ESL High school students and why?
- What do you think would be a good Field Trip for ESL university students and why?
- Have you ever organized a Service Project for your students? If yes, how did you set it up?
- What do you think would be a good Service Project for ESL Elementary school students and why?
- What do you think would be a good Service Project for ESL High school students and why?
- What do you think would be a good Service Project for university level ESL students and why?

Focus on Meaning

Chapter Outline

Vignette

Sherman Elementary School decided to focus their monthly professional development (PD) session for their pre-service ESL teachers in training on the idea of connecting second language lessons to other subject areas these students are studying. The leader of the PD session set up an activity where three pre-service teachers that are assigned to the school for practice teaching, Farah, Ricardo, and Jocelyn, would simulate being math teachers rather than ESL teachers so that they could better appreciate what math teachers must cover and especially what type of language they must use. And so Farah, Ricardo, and Jocelyn, found themselves deep in thought, trying to solve the math problem they were given by the workshop leader. After some time, two of the three pre-service teachers admitted that they could not solve the problem as they had forgotten the formula, and after all they were ESL teachers and not math teachers. However, the workshop leader reminded them that they will encounter such math problems that they will have to explain to their ESL students who may have problems understanding the language attached to the problem if not the problem itself. The problem, as shown below, is not a complex one. Why then could these teachers not solve a simple problem? Here is the problem: *You have taken a loan of $500 for 7 years at a simple interest rate of 12.5% per year. How much interest will you have to pay during the 7 years?* Many adults admit to a drill and rote learning (memorization) approach in their education. Many of us would admit to not remembering the many mathematical formulae that we learned in our mathematics lessons in school or college. Even if we had forgotten the formula for simple interest, would we have been able to solve the problem if we had meaningfully learned the first principle of simple interest? Yes, if learning had been meaningful, we would understand the meaning of "an interest rate of 12.5% per year." We would know,

a. For each $100, the interest per year is $12.50,
b. For $500, the interest per year is $12.50 x 5 = $62.50,
c. For a loan taken for 7 years, the interest is $62.50 x 7 = $437.50.

Hence, even if the formula (principle x rate x time/ 100) is forgotten, we can calculate the interest using our understanding of what simple interest means.

Some people think (at least within behaviorist psychology) that one size fits all for learning; give the same to all students and they will all learn equally – at least that is how it should go, but we teachers know a different reality, one that shows us that each student reacts in a different manner to what is in a text, or on a black/greenboard or an overhead projector. In contrast to the one-size-fits-all metaphor mentioned above, socio-cognitive psychology stresses that people learn by chunking new information with existing knowledge and that meaning plays a key role in forming those chunks. In other words, learning cannot take place in isolation from what learners already know about a topic and meaning provides a purpose for that learning because it enables deeper thinking to take place. Indeed, research on the brain highlights that our brains seek meaning (Jensen, 2008). The German philosopher Nietzsche emphasized that people need to have reasons for what they do, "He [*sic*] who has a Why to live for can bear almost any How." In a book on his experiences as a World War II concentration camp prisoner, Frankl, who was also a psychiatrist, disagrees with Freud's view that humans primarily seek pleasure and with Adler's view that humans' main goal is power. Instead, in *Man's search for meaning* (1959), Frankl argues that our central quest is for meaning.

In the not too distant past, second language education also emphasized drilling and rote memorization of the second language in the hope that some of this would stick in long-term memory. In other words, the idea was that if learners do something often enough, they will remember it. While drills and memorization might be of benefit for short-term language learning, such as providing an answer for a grammar question on past tense construction in a fill-in-the-blank type exercise, long-term learning and the extension of that learning require that students focus on the meaning of the language they are using. In second language education, "meaning" can be understood in terms of the meaning of individual words and whole texts, as well as the meaning that particular topics and events have in students' lives (Halliday & Matthiessen, 1999). As Richards and Rodgers (2001) maintain, in a CLT approach to second language education, "Language is a system for the expression of meaning" (p. 161). The math problem given earlier that the learner ESL teachers are trying to solve needs language to explain its meaning, and that is why it is important that these teachers are able to explain how to solve the problem to their ESL students using the target language. We see many examples of how drill and rote learning leads to less than effective learning not just in mathematics education (as in part of the example above), but in all fields of education, including second language education. This chapter outlines and discusses the essential Focus on Meaning within a CLT approach to second language education and suggests that second language teachers can actively implement more student collaboration in their classes so that the students can further develop their second language skills and abilities.

Focus on meaning

Underpinning the view of learning for understanding is the central role that learners play in constructing their own knowledge. Constructivists (as opposed to behaviorists) view learning not as a passive process of absorbing information transmitted by a teacher. Rather, learners actively seek to make sense of new experiences and new information through the filter of their purposes, interests, prior experiences, and knowledge. Language plays a crucial role in this process. As Powell and Caseau (2004) maintain,

> The relationship between learning and language is at the core of constructivist approaches to education. . . . the belief that learners construct their own meaning from interaction with texts, problems, materials, students, teachers, and other features of the learning environment. (p. 8)

So rather than knowledge being something independent of the knowers, something that is the same for everyone, learners' active personal construction of meaning determines the sense made of any situation. As we interact with our environment, there is constant active construction of meaning which may be modified in the light of new purposes, experiences, and knowledge. As educators, regardless of our subject specialization, learning should be seen as a process of knowledge generation by learners whose prior knowledge is elaborated and changed as a result of their interactions with us, their peers, others, and their environment. Table 5.1 highlights the key differences between the behaviorist and constructivist classroom.

Table 5.1 Behaviorist and constructivist classroom

Behaviorist	Constructivist
Knowledge imparted from teacher to learner	Knowledge constructed by learner based on prior experience and understanding
Learning is observable changes in behaviors	Learning is the search for meaning by linking prior knowledge with new experiences. Meaning implies understanding parts in context of wholes.
	Learning occurs with the learners' understanding continually undergoing construction and reconstruction
Learners are passive, listening to teacher, note-taking and completing worksheets – rote and memorization	Learners are active, doing inquiry-based investigations individually or in cooperative groups with self-reflection
Teachers are active, dominate through exposition	Teachers are facilitators and co-constructors of knowledge with learners through inquiry
More covered but rote learning leads to less effective learning – short term benefit	Less covered but learned meaningfully with understanding – long term benefit

Within second language education, we see many examples of a shift toward emphasizing meaning and understanding that is the core of the CLT approach. In CLT, the focus lies in using language, not in language usage (Breen & Candlin, 1980), such as in the story in the introduction to this chapter where the learner ESL teachers realized that they had to use the language to explain the math problem just as their second language students would also have to use the language to explain how to solve the math problem. Thus, fluency rather than accuracy is prioritized; we are not trying to get our second language students to be grammatically correct with each sentence, rather, we are trying to get them to use whatever knowledge of the second language they have to explain the math problem. For example, when the ESL learner teachers in the above story interact with their students (or when students interact with each other), rather than making immediate corrections of language errors, the learner ESL teachers are encouraged to focus on the meaning and only to interrupt if they think the meaning is being lost, obscured, or imperiled by students' language errors. Yes, feedback on usage (accuracy) remains important, but is not always the first priority within a Focus on Meaning essential in second language education (Richards & Rodgers, 2001).

Classroom implications

Task-based language teaching

Within a Focus on Meaning approach to second language education we can find some general classroom applications such as Task-Based Language Teaching (Long & Crookes, 1992) that emphasize meaning by stressing that students are using language to achieve a purpose. Even though recent years have seen a greater role for explicit grammar instruction, this explicit instruction still takes place within the context of whole texts, i.e., beginning with an understanding of the text and its communicative intent, then looking at how the grammar aids the accomplishment of that intent within the specific context from which that intent derived (Long, 1991). A simple example would be that if speakers' task is to recount a past event, they might want to use the past tense.

Long (1997) emphasizes that tasks should be authentic. While there are many definitions of "authentic," one definition of this term is that the tasks students do in class should mirror the kinds of tasks they are or might be doing in the world outside. For example, students interested in online gaming could play such games, discuss them, write about them, etc. all in the target language. Another example of an authentic task could be students who are looking for a part-time job could work on a job application. This meaning of authenticity links with a core concept in the chapter on Integrated Curriculum that education should connect with students' lives. Therefore, what counts as authentic would vary depending on the learners' context.

Here, with this definition of authenticity, we also see another sense of the term "meaning" as used in this chapter's element. For learning activities to hold meaning for students requires more than students knowing the definitions of the vocabulary they are using. Meaning also involves activities being meaningful to students' lives.

Tasks are defined as "activities in which language is used for carrying out meaningful tasks to promote learning" (Richards and Rodgers, 2001, p. 72). As such, Task-Based Language Teaching (TBLT) is supposed to develop students' communicative competence, a cornerstone of CLT. Thus the mergence of "TBLT is a recent extension of traditional CLT" (Richards and Rodgers, 2001, p. 224). We use Nunan's (2004) definition of a pedagogical task as "a piece of classroom work that involves learners in comprehending, manipulating, producing, or interaction in the target language while their attention is principally focused on mobilizing their grammatical knowledge in order to express meaning, and in which the intention is to convey meaning rather than to manipulate form" (p. 4), for the tasks students can complete in a CLT approach to second language education. For example, Feez and Joyce (1998) suggest that successful implementation of the text-based approach must go through five phases in which the teacher and students work together at understanding text-types:

- *Phase 1:* Build the context, i.e., students build their knowledge of the topic they are going to be exploring through language.
- *Phase 2:* Model and deconstruct the text, i.e., students examine one or more samples of texts (spoken or written) in the content area and the text type, and seek to understand the purpose, organization, and language features (e.g., tenses, connectors, specific vocabulary).
- *Phase 3:* Joint construction of the text, i.e., students cooperate with the teacher and/or partners to create texts in the same text type and content area.
- *Phase 4:* Independent construction of the text, i.e., students work alone to create their own texts with feedback from peers and teachers.
- *Phase 5:* Linking to related texts.

The whole idea of TBLT is that both teachers and students are working together in completing a task. This is especially true where Feez and Joyce (1998) outline what can happen in phase 3 above – joint construction activities:

- o Teacher questioning, discussing, and editing during whole class construction of a text, then scribing onto board, computer or OHT.
- o Skeleton texts – an outline of a text; students use their content knowledge and their knowledge of the text type to fill out the skeleton.
- o Jigsaw and information gap activities – Jigsaw is a well-known cooperative learning technique (see more on cooperative learning in the chapter on The Social Nature of Learning); information gap tasks provide each learner with unique information which must be shared in order for the task to be completed.
- o Small group construction of texts – in which students work in pairs to recon-struct a text that has been read aloud to them. This is not a word-for-word reconstruction, but one which is faithful to the meaning of the text and its text type.
- o Dictogloss (Jacobs & Small, 2003).
- o Self-assessment and peer assessment activities.

Building meaningful vocabulary

While the brain understands in multiple ways, especially for academic purposes, words are essential for making meaning, whether in language class or elsewhere. For instance, Holliday (1991) estimates that a high school chemistry text might contain as many as 3,000 new vocabulary items – more than most students learn in a year in a foreign language class. How can this vocabulary learning be done meaningfully? First, words can be learned by means other than other words. Thus, definitions and written explanations aren't the only means. For example, visuals and demonstrations can also be used. For instance, students can create concept maps that show new vocabulary and concepts in their natural networked state.

Figure 5.1 presents a concept map of how energy cycles.

Second, games can engage students and help them understand new terms. These are not games for games sake, although having fun is a worthy goal. For instance, students can play the game *Twenty Questions* using terms that they have encountered in their studies. Furthermore, games can be played cooperatively, rather than games always being about competition. With a cooperative perspective, the game derives meaning not just from the vocabulary but also from the effort to support one's groupmates.

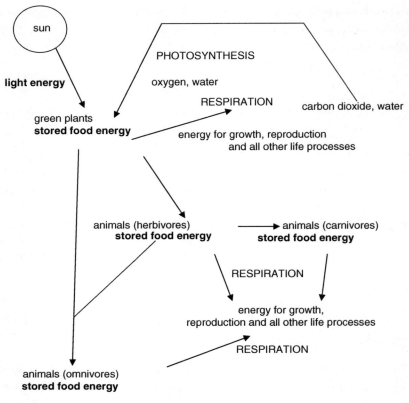

Figure 5.1 Concept map of energy cycle

A third way that learning vocabulary can be meaningful is via writing. Students need to be able to understand meaning and to create meaning that others can understand. Just being able to recall the composition of a chemical compound or just remembering the date of an important historical event has little value without a deeper understanding of the meaning behind these facts. The point is that understanding involves more than just knowing something or even being able to do something. It is a bit like the insightful reply we once heard from a teacher in response to the sarcastic line that "Those who can do, those who can't teach." This teacher replied, "Those who only can, do. Those who also understand, teach."

Too often, students have read the homework assignment or listened to the teacher explain something, but it was in one ear/eye and out the other. Unless they have opportunities to grapple with, apply, explain, and teach, they are not likely to understand. This is one area where the concept of *Writing to Learn* can be valuable. One form of writing to learn involves response journals which students write as they read material or during and after a class. Examples would be good here.

Inquiry

Constructivism provides the philosophical basis for *inquiry-based teaching and learning*. In *inquiry-based learning*, also known as *problem-based learning*, questions arise out of students' experience and interests. In other words, the questions and problems are meaningful to students. They can start with one question but develop others while investigating the initial question. A non-linear, recursive activity cycle – similar to the Action Research cycle (see chapter on Teachers as Co-learners) is involved in which students

Ask – Investigate – Create – Discuss – Act – Communicate – Reflect

This cycle is nonlinear and recursive because the various steps can happen many different times and at many different points in the cycle. We see many examples of what happens in drill and rote learning without understanding the basics. For instance, young children can often recite their timetables without any meaningful understanding. When children have no understanding of sets or the concept of multiplication as repeated addition, they are unable to figure out the answer when they are unable to remember what they have rote learned. Children who have understood the meaning of 4×3 will know that it represents three sets of four objects per set, making a total of 12 objects. Hence, if the children forget what has been rote learned for 3×5, they can figure it out by representing and counting the number of objects in five sets of three objects per set. Once grasped, this understanding can then be put to use to answer questions and solve problems.

Tell/rephrase

When we ask students if something is clear, some will invariably nod their heads in the affirmative, but if we ask them to summarize and explain, these same students are many times at a loss and this is very true for second language students. Oftentimes, students really do not understand, but even when they do understand, second language students do not know how to put their understanding into words. Swain (1999) who developed the Output Hypothesis, believes that, "Students gain insights into their own linguistic shortcomings and develop strategies for solving them by working through them with a partner" (p. 145). Tell/Rephrase is part of a family of cooperative techniques that encourage students to listen carefully to what others say and to express that same meaning in other words or to go beyond the meaning expressed. The following steps can be a useful guide for teachers wishing to implement this activity:

- *Step 1*: One member of a group of two or more makes a statement, e.g., "Humans have much longer intestines than do animals who eat meat. Animals who eat meat are called carnivores. Carnivores' shorter intestines allow meat to pass out of their bodies before it can cause harm."
- *Step 2*: Another member of the group attempts to paraphrase the previous statement, e.g., "You stated that our intestines are much longer than the intestines of animals who eat other animals. These animals' shorter intestines are useful, because the meat they eat leaves their bodies quickly without hurting the animals' health."
- *Step 3*: The original speaker (or another group member) says whether the paraphrase was adequate, e.g., "Yes, that is what I meant." If it wasn't the original speaker and the *reteller* try again.
- *Step 4*: The *rephraser* makes a statement, e.g., "However, humans only have one stomach, whereas cows (who are herbivores) have four stomachs," and pattern of statement/paraphrase/statement/paraphrase continues.
- *Step 5*: The teacher may call on a few students to summarize some of their group's discussion.

There are many variations on Tell/Rephrase. Here are just a few:

- *Tell/Repeat*: Students try to repeat what their partner has said. *Tell/Disagree*: In addition to or instead of rephrasing, a partner can disagree with the first speaker's statement.
- *Tell/Exemplify*: The second speaker can demonstrate their understanding by giving an example of what the previous speaker said.
- *Tell/Generalize*: Instead of being more specific, the second speaker makes a statement at a higher level of generality, e.g., if the first person talked about asking people to sign a petition, the second group member could talk about ways to make ones' voices heard.
- *Tell/Spin Off*: The second speaker takes one idea from what the first said and transfers it to another context or otherwise extends it in some way.
- *Tell/Vary*: The second speaker shows another way to do the same task, such as the same math problem, or to express the same ideas.

Helping students find meaning in the curriculum

As is discussed in detail in the chapter on the element of Learner Autonomy, students learn best when they feel they have some power over and responsibility for their own learning. In this way, students can better craft and grasp the meaning of the curriculum in which they are participating. Equipped with this meaning students are better prepared to understand what they are doing in class and why they are doing. This should not only boost learning but also prepare students to be life-long learners.

Role of teachers

When our second language students are struggling or seem uninterested, teachers need to resist the powerful temptation to jump in and explain concepts. Everyone involved might think that such interventions improve the situation. The teachers have done their jobs – teaching = talking – and students have done theirs – learning = listening attentively to teachers. However, constructivism makes clear that such a transmission model just does not work and this is especially true for second language students. Along with the metaphor of construction of knowledge is another metaphor from building, the idea of *scaffolding*. This involves providing support for learners as they go about constructing their own knowledge. Teachers can provide support, as can peers. Textbooks too can play an important role in helping students construct knowledge and these must be chosen carefully by teachers. Current second language textbooks provide many forms of scaffolding for learners. These include pre-reading information and activities that can make reading passages more comprehensible, hands-on activities, graphic organizers, open-ended questions, experiential tasks, and summaries and text features (such as bold type) that highlight key ideas. Furthermore, textbooks are often accompanied by VCDs and other media that offer video, animation, and other aids to learning. That said, even the best textbook has inherent limitations, as due to the need to serve a general audience and the fact that it is out-of-date before it is even printed, it cannot possibly meet the needs of students in a particular place and time. Thus, students and teachers need to search beyond the textbook for a diverse range of resources. This can provide a range of perspectives. Authentic sources, when understandable, are best, as they often have greater meaning for students.

Role of students

Inquiry extends beyond observations, asking questions, data collection, analyses and interpretation, inference, testing explanations against current scientific knowledge, predictions and communications to the processes of problem solving using critical and logical thinking. Thus, in an inquiry driven classroom, learners should be actively engaged in working to construct their own understanding by making connections between facts, questioning, analyzing, interpreting, predicting, thinking and communicating with peers, teachers, and others. In the final analysis, inquiry is as much an attitude toward learning as it is a way of going about learning.

Conclusion

Underlying this shift from a view of learning as drill and memorization to one based on meaning is the shift from a behaviorist to a socio-cognitive framework. Socio-cognitivists believe that each person *constructs* their own understanding of reality in tandem with their environment, and that other humans are the most important elements of that environment. Thus, socio-cognitivists are also known as constructivists or generativists. This chapter has outlined various ways second language teachers can implement an *inquiry* approach into their teaching. The question remains however as to the relevance of rote learning within second language because many approaches to second language education that emphasize rote memorization of isolated vocabulary and drilling of grammar rules remain very popular in many parts of the world today. However, a Focus on Meaning approach to second language education de-emphasizes memorization and drilling and understanding is paramount that recognizes that learning takes place in context, students can transfer what they have learned from one context to another, students discover for themselves, even if what they are discovering is something that others already know, and transmission of information from teachers to students is not the preferred way of learning.

Reflections

- Underlying this shift from a view of learning as drill and memorization to one based on meaning is the shift from a behaviorist to a socio-cognitive framework. Which framework do you support for second language learning and why?

- Underpinning the view of learning for understanding is the central role that learners play in constructing their own knowledge. What would a constructivist ESL classroom that focuses on student understanding look like to you?
- Reflect on how you learned in school. What is an example of a meaningful learning experience you took part in? What is an example of a rote learning experience? Which type of experience was most common?
- Is there a place for rote learning? Or can all learning be meaningful?
- How did you learn a second language in school? Did you memorize or use any meaning approaches such as inquiry?
- Is there a place for rote learning in second language education? Or can all learning be meaningful?
- If you say yes to the first part of the previous question, where do you think rote learning in second language education is useful?
- Given that many of your students probably learned many things in their own education using rote memory (e.g., multiplication tables) how would you go about explaining and implementing a Focus on Meaning approach in your ESL classes?
- What do you think of the introductory story to this chapter? Do you know how to solve such a math problem and how would you explain it to ESL students?
- This chapter suggests that fluency is emphasized over accuracy in a Focus on Meaning approach. Why do you think this would be a good idea or a bad idea?

6 Celebrate Diversity

Vignette

Hee Soon Park is a Korean born naturalized US citizen teaching ESL in a junior high school in the US. Because she moved to the U.S. when she was a child, she does not remember much about her early childhood in Korea but she was constantly reminded of her "different" facial appearance from Caucasian classmates during her grade school years in the U.S. So she is very interested in inclusiveness in her ESL classes and sees that mix of ESL students of different ethnic, religious, social, and economic backgrounds in her classes as a plus rather than a minus because she uses the mix of cultures and different first language backgrounds as lessons for all the students. When she plans her classes she keeps her students' varied interests and abilities in mind. Furthermore Hee Soon knows her students learn in different ways and some of her students are fast language learners but others need more time. Hee Soon also realizes that boys and girls in her classes approach their learning in different ways. In addition, Hee Soon scans whatever materials the department (or school district) wants her to cover in her classes for possible cultural biases and when she finds any, she brings this to the attention of her supervisors. So Hee Soon is a second language teacher who tries to accommodate all her students' differences and similarities under the umbrella term of Diversity as she tries to vary her instructional approaches to address the different ways her students learn a second language. Plus, Hee Soon seeks to create an inviting environment for all students by watching out for anything in materials which might inadvertently lead to an unfriendly environment for some of her students.

In general education, "Diversity" has different meanings for different people and situations. In second language education, we see Diversity in the mix of second language students we have in our classrooms in terms of backgrounds, e.g., ethnic, religious, social class and first language, sex and gender, sexual orientation, achievement levels, learning styles, intelligences and use of learning strategies. We noted in Chapter 2 that a key tenet of learner-centered instruction is that each learner is different and that effective second language teaching should not only celebrate these differences but also take these differences into account when preparing lesson plans, activities, and materials. Hee Soon in the opening vignette of this chapter is one such teacher because she continuously attempts to observe, accommodate, and build on the Diversity of her second language students.

Diversity as it is outlined and discussed in this chapter means that teachers (and students) recognize and celebrate that each of our second language students is unique, and that while all humans share many characteristics, each student and each group of students is unique. We maintain that Diversity and thus student uniqueness is about

- Understanding that second language learners differ in such matters as personality, intelligence profile, learning style, ethnicity, race, religion, sexual orientation, nationality, social class, and physical and mental abilities.
- We must create an environment where all second language students feel respected and welcomed in our community and classes so that we can promote the worth of all of our students.
- We must be aware of the wide range of learning styles and be attentive to these as much as possible so we can encourage second language students to try out different ways of learning depending on how comfortable they are with any changes.
- We must help second language students appreciate the benefits of working toward common goals with people different from themselves so that our classes are examples of places where cultural differences are respected and our students are made aware of ways of communicating between these different people and within cultures.

The chapter outlines and discusses the essential concept of Diversity within a CLT approach to second language education and suggests how second language teachers can actively implement this concept in their classes so that second language students can further develop their language skills and abilities.

Diversity

As mentioned above the term Diversity means different things to different people and we recognize this; however, we focus our discussion on Diversity in this chapter by suggesting that second language teachers consider Diversity from the following perspectives: teacher awareness, learning styles, communication styles, multiple intelligences, and cross-cultural communication. We feel this focus will help second language teachers better accommodate the essential of Diversity within a CLT approach to second language education.

Teacher awareness

We suggest that any discussion of Diversity start with second language teachers in that we need to become more aware of who we are as people and second language teachers. As people, we language teachers need to develop a critical level of awareness of who we are in terms of our own background influences such as our race, ethnicity, gender, and socioeconomic backgrounds. This awareness allows us to understand how people's background affects who they are, what they do, and how they feel about themselves and others. Equipped with this growing understanding, we are better prepared to gain insight into our students and how they too are affected by their backgrounds. Also, as we become more aware of the effects of background, we can see how we may have become biased in our perceptions and practices over our careers and how these may have influenced our teaching although we may not have realized this. As Sleeter, Torres, and Laughlin (2004) maintain, teachers need to develop "a critical consciousness of their own reality as persons of a specific race, ethnicity, gender, and socioeconomic status, with specific abilities, and stories" (p. 84).

However, it may not be easy for teachers to become aware of possible biases because over the years we build up a wall between our inner selves and outer performances so that we can forget who we really are. So, Palmer (cited in Farrell, 2007) urges all teachers to "ask the 'who' question – who is the self that teaches?" (p. 5). Farrell (2007) proposes that second language teachers can become more aware of who they are as teachers by articulating their stories to themselves or others because these stories reveal the experiences that guide their work. By telling their stories, Farrell (2007) maintains that teachers can make better sense of seemingly random experiences because we hold the inside knowledge, especially personal intuitive knowledge, expertise, and experience that is based on our accumulated years as language educators and students, teaching and learning in schools and classrooms. In this way then second language teachers can become aware of their past influences and can thus be better placed when attempting to accommodate the needs, different learning preferences, and styles of their students.

Learning styles

Learning styles can be defined as "distinctive behaviors that serve as indicators of how a person learns from and adapts to his [sic] environment" (Gregorc, 1979, p. 234). When second language teachers examine the concept of learning styles, their own and those of their students, they come to realize that everyone has a learning style; however, they may not be able to articulate this style to others. For example, some students think in a linear, step-by-step way while others like to chunk their thoughts holistically. However, second language teachers must remember learning styles are unique to individuals and are a "biologically and developmentally imposed set of characteristics that make the same teaching method effective for some and ineffective for others" (Dunn, Beaudry, & Klaves, 1989, p. 50). Thus second language teachers may need to modify their instruction to accommodate different learning styles by realizing that not all our language students learn best while sitting at a desk, or in a quiet setting, or even through group instruction. Indeed we must realize that some of our students may be field-dependent second language learners and thus need to be immersed in the second language, while others are field-independent because they focus more on the details of the language they are learning and look at its structure independent of its use in society. In terms of learning modality preferences, some of our students may be visual learners and thus may like to see patterns, pictures, shapes, while other students may be more auditory learners and like to listen and talk and even sing while learning, yet other learners are tactile (or kinesthetic) type learners and as such like more hands-on activities such as role plays, body movements, and gesture a lot while speaking the second language. So language teachers face the constant challenges of helping students become aware of their learning styles and then trying to accommodate these different styles in their classrooms. Second language teachers can try to respond to these differences by using a variety of teaching methods and grouping patterns.

Communication styles

Hymes' (1972) work on communicative competence, a key facet of CLT's foundation, includes the role of culture and people from different cultures that view the world differently and that these differences have an impact on communication style (Heath, 1983). Teachers should realize that second language students interpret classroom activities through their own frames of reference (Farrell, 2007), which are sometimes different because all our students have different experiences and background knowledge which in turn is different to the teacher's background. In second language education, students already face the difficulty of communicating in a new language. This difficulty is compounded when students' learned ways of talking and other forms of language use do not conform to the patterns of communication expected in classrooms and may, therefore, be misunderstood and unappreciated. Second language educators need to be aware of this and attempt to come to understand and appreciate their students' frames of reference. For example, teachers must realize that their own behavior in their classroom is affected by their own background and as such we should be aware that some of our cultural norms may differ a lot from our students' cultures. Language teachers can become more aware of their students' cultures by making a conscious effort to learn more about their students' home–family relationships, their community culture, and their cultural heritage. Language teachers can augment this by looking for cultural bias in textbooks and curricular materials to see if they contain any distortions about minority cultures or ethnic groups.

Multiple intelligences

Connected to the fact that our students have different learning styles is the view that intelligence is composed of a mixture of nature and nurture, or heredity and experience. Furthermore, intelligence had previously been viewed as a unitary construct. Today, the more dominant view sees intelligence as more varied, as plural, intelligences, not singular. Gardner's Multiple Intelligences theory is probably the best-known theory espousing this view. Gardner theory states that every person has distinctive sets of capabilities and inclinations that all work together. In its present form, the theory identifies eight different intelligences:

- *Verbal-linguistic* – Thinking in words; learning through reading, writing, listening, and talking.
- *Logical-mathematical* – Thinking in numbers and patterns; learning through problem-solving, symbols, and analysis.
- *Visual-spatial* – Thinking in pictures and images; learning through visualizing, drawing, and creating graphic organizers, such as mind maps and tables.
- *Musical-rhythmic* – Thinking in rhythm, lyrics, and melody; learning through music, chants, and poetry and the words that accompany them.
- *Bodily-kinesthetic* – Using the whole body or parts of the body to solve problems, make things, and demonstrate ideas; learning through hands-on activities and role play.
- *Naturalist* – Being aware of and interested in nature; learning by classifying and observing nature and other phenomena, including people and people-made objects.
- *Intrapersonal* - Feeling comfortable with oneself and understanding oneself; learning by taking time to reflect and consider the relevance of ideas for oneself.
- *Interpersonal* – Understanding and respecting others; learning by discussing, explaining, asking, and debating with others.

The implication of the presence of multiple intelligences for second language teachers is that instruction must be varied so that in a particular unit, at different times, each student gets a match with the intelligences in which they most prefer to operate. Each student gets stretched by working with intelligences in which they are less developed and students come to appreciate the value of working with people of varied intelligence profiles. Additionally, by being aware of the different intelligence profiles of themselves, their classmates, their teachers, and others and by appreciating the benefits of learning with people of different profiles, students celebrate Diversity.

Cross-cultural communication

Diversity means difference and that we humans are not all the same and we may not all have the same common style and patterns of communications of the majority within a culture. This is especially true in second language education where many of our students come from different ethnic, social, political, occupational, religious backgrounds and beliefs, not to mention different geographical backgrounds. This is a real challenge for second language teachers because we may not knowingly practice discrimination against some of our students unless we become knowledgeable in how to communicate cross-culturally and thus respect human rights and Diversity. One way of becoming proficient in cross-cultural communication is by becoming more aware of what prejudice is and then trying to avoid prejudging in teaching.

According to the Alberta Human Rights Commission (1978) prejudice is "an attitude or belief formed or held without really considering the facts. It is for or against something or someone" (p. 6). Taken in its negative form then ("against") unfortunately in today's world we have racial profiling that is very prejudicial against certain races; for example, if one has a name that originated in the Middle East, travel in North America can be difficult. In second language education, teachers must become aware of any negative "prejudging" attitudes they may have in teaching certain ethnic groups. Once we are aware of such attitudes, we need to try to avoid any preconceived notions we may have because they can have many negative consequences for our students and ourselves. Teachers must also become aware of positive ("for" in the above definition) because these may put unfair expectations on that ethnic group; for example, we may assume that our Japanese second language students are always polite and rarely question what others are doing, but what will we think if one Japanese second language student begins to question our teaching methods? Will we think less of this student because of our preconceived notions of how a Japanese student *should* act? Will we react differently if a student from North America questions our teaching methods? Consequently we must become aware of our prejudices and be careful that we do not discriminate (according to the Alberta Human Rights Commission, discrimination is "prejudice transmitted into action" (p. 6) against any of our students. Teachers can also help their students and themselves by teaching their students about cultural Diversity.

Classroom implications

Spot the difference

Many well-established second language teaching techniques can be used to tap a range of intelligences. For example, *Spot the Difference* is a technique which taps students' naturalist intelligence, discussed above. As students work in pairs, each has a different item, for instance, one has a detailed anatomical drawing of a butterfly and the other a drawing of a grasshopper, or one has an advertisement written to appeal to teenagers and the other has an advertisement for the same product but written to appeal to people in their twenties. The two students do not show each other their materials. Instead, they carefully describe the materials to their partner and identify the similarities and differences. *Spot the Difference* promotes attention to detail and careful observation, proclivities of people who enjoy using their Naturalist intelligence. Other uses of *Spot the Difference* include comparing two versions of the same story, two countries, or two paragraphs with different grammatical structures.

Think/write time

Connected to intrapersonal intelligence discussed above, we realize that some of our second language students may need some time before speaking in the second language to their groupmates, the whole class, or the teacher. We remember that Diversity means that not all our students learn in the same way or at the same pace and as such, more time is given for these students to think about what they are going to say before they say it. We can accommodate this by telling them that we will give them a few minutes to think about what they want to say and say nothing until our students speak, or we can ask them to write out what they want to say before they say it. This extra time helps students develop the propensity to think on their own. The advantage of Write time is that it is easier for students to share with others what they have written than what they have said.

Charades and role play

When students use their physical as well as their mental energies in learning and sharing their learning, bodily-kinesthetic intelligence comes to the fore. Charades offers one means of getting students out of their seats and moving more than their mouths. Even more simply, students can use their hands, etc. to represent individual vocabulary items. Indeed, almost any concept can be captured in some gesture, hand symbol, or other type of body movement. Another opportunity for students to move around is when they participate in role play, which can also involve charades.

Bloom in group discussions

One reason group discussions in many second language classrooms end as quickly as they begin is that both teachers and students take a *closed approach* to accomplishing set tasks because as Barnes (1976) maintains, "The group finds nothing to encourage active engagement, nothing to provoke questions or surmises" (p. 38). A *closed approach* to discussions within a group limits investigations and exploration of issues because probing questions that underlie an issue are not asked. Bloom's Taxonomy (Bloom, 1956) of Thinking Skills is very useful for guiding second language students during group discussions especially when they want to apply, and synthesize information in order to create something from that information (see also Chapter 7 on Thinking Skills for more details). For example, if students want to analyze information in a group they can break down the information into its component parts by first discussing this as a group. They can then synthesize this information by formulating a new plan, and further evaluating this plan by judging the value of the ideas generated by the group and then deciding on a course of action agreed upon by each group member. This type of process can be represented as follows:

- *Analyze* – Break down information into parts by group discussion and make lists of the parts.
- *Synthesize* – Put together the ideas/parts into a new plan by group discussion.
- *Evaluate* – Evaluate the merit of the ideas/materials based on an agreed (by group) set of standards in the form of group discussion/ debate.

- *Apply* – This plan can be put into action by using the new accepted ideas/materials in new situations.

Thus various Thinking Skills are called into play as students attempt to explain concepts and procedures to their group members, as group members give each other feedback, and as they debate the proper course of action. Because of the absence of the teacher in group discussions, the students themselves must initiate, respond, and in certain cases evaluate and/or acknowledge responses and initiations made by other group participants. As mentioned above, group work does not mean a complete absence of the teacher. In fact, the teacher remains central to the success of group work and project work (Gillies, 2007). The teacher can influence the success of the group by making sure that the task undertaken is appropriate, and that the students all know what is expected from them during group work. The teacher may also want to monitor group discussions because these discussions may remain at the superficial level or they may not be able to conclude successfully if they have no guidelines to follow for the discussions.

Thinking Skills also come into play in terms of another meaning of Diversity. This involves diverse answers to the same question, diverse solutions to the same problem, and diverse questions and problems in search of answers and solutions. Thinking is a messy process, and this messiness must not only be allowed; it must be encouraged. Based on their different backgrounds, students will come to classroom tasks from different perspectives, and the value of this difference should be appreciated. For example, rather than looking only for the answer we expect to a question we've asked, teachers should encourage a range of answers.

Spot the bias

Most teachers use particular materials and textbooks in class to teach a particular concept or language point. However, many teachers do not realize or take the time to consider that some of these materials and texts may contain certain bias or distortions about particular ethnic groups (Byrnes & Kiger, 2005). We can guard against this by looking for some of the following misrepresentations:

- *Omission of relevant facts* – leaving out relevant facts about particular groups.
- *Defamation* – only looking at groups' faults in stereotypical ways that portrays the group in overly negative ways.
- *Validity* – the information about a group is incorrect, or invalid, because it is not accurate, or up to date for whatever reason.

Build cultural respect

Second language teachers respect human rights and differences and celebrate these multiple diversities so that we can fully implement the CLT approach in second language education by trying to establish *cultural respect* in their classes. This can be achieved by asking each student to research their family background and then have them present their findings to the class. This can include details of not only their particular family backgrounds, but also the cultural backgrounds in terms of literature, music, art. If time permits, students can present the music and art of their culture to the class. Also, if musicians and/or artists from a particular culture live in the community, they could be invited to give talks and perform for the class and/or the school.

Role of teachers

Second language teachers need to understand the varied characteristics of both themselves and their students and look for ways to help all students learn. First, teachers need to develop a sense of self and an examination of their own ethnic and cultural identity to see if they have any hidden bias against any ethnocultural groups. Next, they need to learn about their students in terms of their backgrounds and their learning modalities and preferences. Second language teachers can accommodate Diversity in their classes by addressing the following:

- Become clear of own (teacher's) ethnic and cultural identity.
- Establish own attitudes towards other ethnic and culture groups.
- Become familiar about all prejudice and racism and avoid in classes.
- Discover relationships between language, culture, and second language learning.
- Learn about learning styles of various ethnic groups and try to accommodate these different learning styles.
- Get to know all students as individuals and not as a representative of a particular ethnic group.
- Use instructional materials that reflect diverse cultural backgrounds.

Role of students

Students too have a role in accommodating Diversity in their learning. For example, students need to respect and welcome *all* their classmates irrespective of where they come from geographically or politically and despite the differences that may exist between them. In addition, all students, regardless of who they are, should be able to see themselves in the materials used in class. This will undoubtedly mean going beyond the materials found in textbooks. For instance, the languages and non-standard dialects of students should appear in materials. Students should make teachers aware of any bias they may see in textbooks and material rather than resenting these materials. So students can help play the role of teacher too and show their classmates how these materials are biased against a particular ethnic group.

Conclusion

This chapter on the essential of teaching for Diversity recognizes that within all classroom activities we second language teachers need to strive for classrooms in which students can be their unique selves without fear of derision or exclusion, in which difference can be appreciated rather than demeaned. Language and identity are inextricably mixed. This is why a school can be a place of alienation for those students who do not speak the standard variety of the language of instruction which, for example, in the U.S. is Standard English. Yes, students need to know this standard in order to succeed in academia, but we want to strive for an additive abroad to language in which students who speak different dialects or languages add Standard English to what they already speak, rather than a subtractive approach in which students replace their mother tongue with Standard English. So we second language teachers have an important role to play to ensure that Diversity is accommodated in our classes as we implement a CLT approach within second language education.

Reflections

- What does the term "Diversity" mean to you?
- What is your particular learning style and can you see any signs of this style being represented in your instructional materials?
- As a result of this reflection do you think your instructional materials may be biased towards to your preferred learning style rather than those of your students?
- Do you check the instructional materials you use for bias against any ethnic groups? How do you check the materials you use for these biases?

- Looking at the different ways teachers can spot the bias in textbooks and materials discussed above, do you implement any of these now?
- Can you think of other ways second language teachers can spot the biases in materials to accommodate Diversity in their classes?
- Looking at the different roles of the teacher discussed above, do you implement any of these particular roles in your classes at the moment?
- Can you think of other roles second language teachers should implement to accommodate Diversity in their classes?
- Recall a time when, either as a student or a teacher, you witnessed an incident in which a minority student was made to feel unwelcome in a classroom or elsewhere in a school. How did the teacher and others react? Do you have any suggestions for how they might have reacted better to the incident?
- The teacher for this class in Japan came up with some very inventive ways of helping her students (the roles and the clapping) to help expand the group discussions. When she did have to intervene she said that she consciously attempted to limit her utterances and avoid evaluations by reacting to the content of the discussion. What do you think of this type of intervention? How do you intervene in group discussions?

Expand Thinking Skills

Vignette

Mrs. Haley teaches in an elementary school and she has noticed that some of her 4th graders continue to struggle with the language demands of their mainstream classes, especially science class. Mrs. Haley has analyzed the science textbook and with the help of a linguistics book, she has determined that one of the main academic language functions that is typical of science texts that is especially challenging for ESL students is expressing cause and effect, i.e. what will happen if and when X happens or why something happens. Mrs. Haley decided to plan a lesson focusing on this problematic language function by presenting it in the context of the science textbook. Mrs. Haley first decided to give her ESL students graphic representations of cause and effect. She then told her students that a useful way of identifying cause-and-effect is by asking questions that have them answer "what happens as a result of an action" and then she explained the action as follows, "I worked out hard every day for six months in preparation for the race." This is a cause statement. The effect, or result, is what happened as a result of the action, such as, "I won the race." She then proceeded with the lesson using the science textbook examples of cause and effect. Mrs. Haley gave directions for her students to work in pairs, and then distributed an activity to each pair. When each pair had completed their activity, she used a general class discussion format for each pair to share their responses. Following this discussion, and other activities, Mrs. Haley was happy that the students had a better idea of cause and effect, and at the end of class she told them that they should try to practice and use this construct in their speech and writing as much as possible so that they will be able to quickly recognize it when they see it in a reading passage in whatever subject they are studying in future. When they "see it" they should write the example in their journals so that they can compare.

The essential of Thinking Skills within a CLT approach to second language education contrasts with rote learning and finding "right there" answers, i.e., answers to comprehension questions in which the answer is right there on the page that students have just read with no real Thinking Skills required. Thinking Skills activities ask students to go beyond the information given, to draw on what they have previously studied, their experiences, their views of the world, their hopes and their thinking strategies. Perhaps the best known taxonomy of Thinking Skills is the one developed back in the 1950s by Bloom and his colleagues. Bloom's Taxonomy consists of six overlapping categories of thinking.

1. *Knowledge* – This category involves students in recalling what has been taught. For example, if students have read a passage about clothing, a *knowledge* question might be, "What color was Manuel's shirt?," when the answer is right there in the text.
2. *Understanding* – This category asks students to demonstrate comprehension of what is being studied. For example, with the same task, an *understanding* task might be to construct a table that includes the people in the text, the clothing they

are wearing and their style preferences. Another understanding task might ask students to retell an incident described in the text.

3. *Application* – This category of thinking involves students in using the ideas/ information in the text to do something or to plan to do something. Examples would be coming to school the next day dressed similarly to one of the people in the text and explaining the similarity, or cutting clothing pictures from magazines or newsletters and using the vocabulary in the text to describe the pictures.

4. *Analysis* – This category in Bloom's Taxonomy is about comparing, contrasting, separating, and examining. For instance, after reading our clothing text, students might want to compare their clothes when they were younger to what they wear today.

5. *Synthesis* – While analysis focuses on the parts, synthesis is about wholes and con-structing. For instance, students might enjoy creating a list of clothing suggestions, with drawing, for what their teachers should wear to school.

6. *Evaluation* – This category of thinking involves students giving opinions, taking positions and doing ratings. An example of this type of thinking related to the clothing text might be to look at pictures of celebrities and rate their clothing on a 5-point scale with reasons given for the ratings.

The point of discussing Bloom's Taxonomy is that too often education used to include only Knowledge and Understanding types of thinking, whereas in the real world students do all types of thinking. Thus, if we want to bring the class-room closer to the real world and prepare students to cope with that world, we need to broaden the type of thinking we encourage and to help students to engage successfully in these many types of cognitive activity. Table 7.1 outlines Bloom's Taxonomy in detail.

This chapter then outlines and discusses the essential of Thinking Skills within a CLT approach to second language education and gives specific examples of how second language teachers can implement Thinking Skills in their classes.

Thinking skills

The essential of Thinking Skills flows from the CLT approach in a few senses. First, thinking is a process and the emphasis lies in the quality of that process rather than solely on the quality of the product resulting from that process. Additionally, Diversity (see previous Chapter 6 for more details on this essen-tial) comes into play, as many valid routes may exist toward thinking about a particular situation or performing a particular task. Another connection

Table 7.1 Bloom's Taxonomy of thinking processes *(adaptation)*

Level of Taxonomy	Definition	Student Roles	Action Verbs
Knowledge	Recall of specific information	responds; absorbs; re-members; recognizes	tell; list; define; name; identify; state; remember; repeat
Comprehension (understanding)	Understanding of communicated information	explains; translates; demonstrates; interprets	Transform; change; restate; describe; explain; review; paraphrase; relate; generalize; infer
Application (using)	Use of rules, concepts, principles and theo-ries in new situations	solves problems; demonstrates; uses knowledge; constructs	apply; practice; employ; use; demonstrate; illustrate; show; report
Analysis (taking apart)	Breaking down infor-mation into parts	discusses; uncovers; lists; dissects	analyze; dissect; distinguish; examine; compare; contrast; survey; investigate; separate; categorize; classify; organize
Synthesis (creating new)	Putting together of ideas into a new or unique plan	discusses; generalizes; relates; contrasts	create; invent; compose; construct; design; modify; imagine; produce; propose; what if…
Evaluation (judging)	Judging the value of materials or ideas on the basis of set standards or criteria	judges; disputes; forms opinions; debates	judge; decide; select; justify; evaluate; critique; debate; verify; recommend; assess

Adapted from Farrell (2006).

between Thinking Skills and the current paradigm is that Learner Autonomy (see Chapter 2 for more details on this essential) is promoted by encouraging students to connect the language learning they do in school with the world beyond. This attempt promotes the idea that learning is not a collection of lower-order facts to be remembered and then regurgitated on exams, but that the aim of school learning is to apply our knowledge toward making a better world.

Connecting education to the wider world in order to improve that world means that students – along with their teachers – need to analyze existing situ-ations, synthesize new ideas, and evaluate proposed alternatives (Freire, 1970).

Certainly, a great deal of higher-order thinking is needed here. For example, if students are studying the water pollution problem mentioned above, they will encounter the kind of tangled thicket of variables that make it so difficult to implement solutions to the mess that humans have made of our planet's environment. Indeed, communicating about global issues, such as environment, peace, human rights and development, requires students to develop and employ their Thinking Skills (Cates & Jacobs, 2006). A trend in this direction can be witnessed by the fact that many organizations of second language educators have subgroups devoted to global issues, e.g., the Global Issues Special Interest Group in IATEFL (International Association of Teachers of English as a Foreign Language http://www.iatefl.org).

Among the many strategies that our students need to acquire and use to succeed in our classes are those that involve going beyond the information given and utilizing and building their Thinking Skills, also known as critical and creative Thinking Skills (Paul & Elder, 2006). Critical thinking for teachers of second or foreign languages generally means educating language students to think about their thinking, its strengths and weaknesses, and then to decide if it needs improvement. Although there seems to be disagreement concerning what actually qualifies as "critical and creative thinking," most educators agree that it includes awareness of standards in abilities and skills, and aspects of student dispositions or attitudes. Both of these can be learned while at the same time recognizing the uniqueness of individual students. In this chapter we define critical thinking as "the intellectually disciplined process of actively and skillfully conceptualizing, applying, analyzing, synthesizing, and/or reasoning, or communication, as a guide to belief and action" (Scriven & Paul, 1987). Critical thinking means getting our students to interpret, analyze, synthesize, argue, reflect on, and evaluate their thoughts, beliefs, and actions to see if they are credible or not.

Critical Thinking Skills can be taught and as such can be learned. Beyer (1984) came up with the following procedures that teachers can emphasize when teaching critical Thinking Skills:

1. Distinguishing between verifiable facts and value claims.
2. Determining the reliability of a claim or source.
3. Determining the accuracy of a statement.
4. Distinguishing between warranted or unwarranted claims.
5. Distinguishing between relevant and irrelevant information, claim, or arguments.
6. Detecting biases.
7. Identifying stated and unstated assumptions.

8. Identifying ambiguous or equivocal claims or arguments.
9. Recognizing logical inconsistencies in a line of reasoning.
10. Determining the strength of an argument. (p. 557)

So the ability to think critically can be taught and learned and can be brought into most discussions in a second language speaking class as well as in most writing assignments. For speaking activities, small groups can engage in problem solving activities by practicing brainstorming on possible answers and then by discussing the reliability and validity of these possible solutions. Second language learners can practice how to disagree, how to challenge, and be challenged. Second language teachers can enhance creative thinking by going on field trips with their students, and/or by inviting expert speakers on specific topics to class so their students can practice exploring their target language skills in situations that get them to stretch their thinking. Second language students can also be encouraged to write journals to help them "see" their thoughts and then to help them take some action in order to again stretch their thinking. Journals offer language students the time for delayed reflection so that they can look back at what happened and then to be able to make informed decisions about the way forward.

This adaptation also suggests the action verbs teachers can adapt when helping second language students access this higher order thinking; for example, at the thinking level of *knowledge* where students are asked to recall specific information by having teachers use action verbs as 'define', 'identify' and the like, the students must remember first and then respond to these teacher solicits; at the *application* level where new concepts are noted teachers ask students to demonstrate their thinking by getting them to solve problems using the new concepts to show they understand how to apply the new concept.

Today, Thinking Skills are seen as an essential part of all aspects of general education, because information is easily obtained, so the essential task is now to use that information wisely. Thinking Skills can be infused into any content, even with students of low L2 proficiency. For example, the teaching of language skills offers many opportunities to infuse Thinking Skills. For example, Early (1990) describes how an ESL instructor teaching basic biology to elementary ESL students used graphic representations of such knowledge structures as the *classification* of types of animal and the *sequence* of the food chain to support student writing, both of which also comprise an academic function. This principle of paying attention to the relationships between knowledge structures that are reflected in the accompanying language functions has instrumental implications for second language instruction. First, in teaching content in a second language it is not enough to teach vocabulary, which seems to be a common practice, because meaning is constructed through knowledge of the *relationships* between forms and vocabulary. It is clear from research that knowing the vocabulary of a text does not equal comprehending the text (e.g. Nation, 2008). It is imperative to teach language functions as well to gain understanding of these relationships. Second, this principle gives support to the assertion that language should be taught contextualized, through meaningful content, because in order to be able to use language, learners need to understand language functions that reflect how language is used.

Classroom implications

We now outline some specific implications that second language teachers can consider when trying encouraging Thinking Skills in their everyday second language classes. Many of these involve group activities. As explored in Chapter 3 on the Social Nature of Learning, interaction provides a venue for sparking students to think more deeply, as peers may ask questions, disagree, provide new insights, and provide assistance.

Question-and-answer pairs

This technique (adapted from Johnson & Johnson, 1999) has the following steps that teachers need to consider when implementing question-and-answer pairs.

- *Step 1* – Both members of a pair of second language students write questions about a particular topic or concept under study. These questions can be of many different types that include review questions or questions about content currently being studied. This is a good opportunity to help students learn how to ask specific thinking questions.
- *Step 2* – Students write answers to their own questions first to make sure they know what they themselves expect in a "correct" answer. With questions that have many possible answers, students can write a model answer.
- *Step 3* – Students exchange questions (all this can happen in class, during class, or electronically from home using computers) but not answers, and then they must attempt to answer each other's questions.

- *Step 4* – Students then compare answers. Part of this comparison involves an important aspect of Thinking Skills and that is the student must state the evidence for their answers. The ideal is for the students to agree on an answer that is better than either of their initial answers thus proving that two heads are better than one.

A variation on Question-and-Answer Pairs is for two pairs to work together in the same way that the two partners work together. First, each pair prepares questions and then writes answers to their own questions. To encourage all group members to be active, each member of the pair writes their own questions and answers before showing them to their partner. Then the pair decides on the best questions and answers. Next, the two pairs exchange questions and create answers to the other pair's questions. Finally, the pairs compare their answers. Just for fun, occasionally students can exchange answers and then try to guess their partner's question as in the game show "Jeopardy." Yet another variation of Question-and-Answer Pairs is for students to write questions for which they do not know the answer. This is a more real world use of the technique, because it is only at school that people ask questions for which they already know the answer. However, students do not just write questions. Even though they do not have answers to their questions, they should write their ideas for what might help toward finding an answer.

Critical writing

Farrell (2006) suggests the following six-stage approach to creative writing that second language teachers can consider within CLT:

- *Stage 1* – Input (Prewriting): Input sessions consist of idea-generating activities to help the students focus on the assignment. Ideas for a topic to write about are generated by one or all of the following means:

  o *Brainstorming.* This is where individuals, pairs, or groups speak or write a number of possible topics and then write them on a piece of paper. Each pair or group reviews the list and, by a process of elimination, arrives at a shortlist of topics to write about; however, the final choice for a specific topic is left to the individual writer.
  o *Free writing.* After brainstorming, students can be encouraged to engage in a period of free writing. Here, the students are required to write as much as possible within a short period of time (usually 15 minutes), without focusing on correctness of grammar, sentence structure, or composition mechanics.

The pairs, groups, and so on, can then read each other's work and advise or suggest an alternative focus for the story, not the grammar.

- *Stage 2* – First Draft: Audience awareness is the focus of this stage, with discussions about the different rhetorical traditions and expectations highlighted. Students are asked to write their first draft at home and further develop the ideas generated in the first stage. Of course, students are free to throw out these ideas for some new focus if they so desire.
- *Stage 3* – Peer Evaluation (Review): Reviewers have a chance to use their knowledge of writing in a way that promotes learning from their own advice. Students should take the advice of their reviewers most of the time and even appreciate the importance of the feedback reviewers provide.
- *Stage 4* – Second Draft: Students are encouraged to make changes in the content (or even start over) as a result of the feedback received in the previous stage. Students are then required to write a second draft at home and bring it to the following class.
- *Stage 5* – Peer Evaluation (Revise): At this stage, peers read again and students are asked to revise again.
- *Stage 6* – Final Draft/Input: The final draft is submitted along with notes from the previous drafts so that students and their teacher can see all the critical thinking and discussions along the way. At this stage of the process, the teacher reads, comments, and returns the composition to the students the following week.

SUMMER

Another communicative language technique that promotes Thinking Skills goes by the acronym of SUMMER. The technique presented in this chapter is slightly adapted from one developed by Donald Dansereau. Here's how this pair technique works:

- **S**et the mood: The pair sets a relaxed, yet purposeful mood. Students can engage in a little chit-chat and also make sure they are clear on the procedure to follow.
- **U**nderstand by reading silently: A reading passage (or section from a textbook) has been divided into sections. (The teacher can do this or students can use natural breaks in the passage, such as chapter sections to divide it.) Each student reads the first section silently.
- **M**ention key ideas: Without looking down at the text, one member of the pair acts as *Recaller*, summarizing the key ideas of the section. Comprehension difficulties can be raised here.
- **M**onitor: The partner looks at the text and acts as Monitor, pointing out any errors, omissions, or unnecessary information in the *Recaller's* summary and praising the *Recaller* for a job well done. The roles of *Recaller* and *Monitor* rotate for the next section.

- **E**laborate: Both students elaborate on the ideas in the section. Types of elaborations include:

  o connections with other things the students have studied
  o links between the section and students' lives
  o additions of relevant information not included in the section
  o agreements or disagreements with views expressed
  o reactions to the section such as surprise, gladness, and anger
  o applications of the ideas and information
  o questions, either about things not understood or questions sparked by the section

Not all types of elaborations are relevant to every section and modifications can be made based on the topic being discussed. Groups repeat the Understand, Recall, Mention, and Elaborate steps for all the sections of the passage.

- **R**eview: The pair combines their thoughts to summarize the entire text.

Clearly, *SUMMER* involves many Thinking Skills. We wouldn't expect students to be good at these skills right away, although it is surprising how many students seem much better at using them in nonacademic contexts. Thus, we need to provide guidance before expecting students to be effective in *SUMMER*. Also, pay attention to the difficulty level of the texts used; how can students summarize and elaborate on a text that they can't understand?

K-W-L

K-W-L (Ogle, 1989) is by now a well-known learning technique, with many variations. Here is one variation, but first let us look at the basic K-W-L version. Table 7.2 is a sample K-W-L table. In the first column, students write what they already know on a topic. This is the K step. This is done alone first, and then students combine knowledge with their groupmates. They also explain the source of their knowledge. Providing sources gives other ideas about where to learn more and raises the issue of what constitutes a trustworthy source. The next step in K-W-L is the W step, in which student, first alone and then in a group, discuss what they want to know about the topic. The step builds students' motivation to learn more related to the topic. The W step also highlights Diversity, because groupmates are likely to want to learn about different aspects of the topic. The third step is the L step, in which students record and report to each other on what they learned. They can also explain to each other

Table 7.2 KWL

What I/We Know	What I/We Want to Know	What I/ We Learned	What I/We Still Want to Know

where they learned this new information. Even if students all read the same text, it can build their reading comprehension to discuss what they learned and where they learned.

A somewhat new twist on K-W-L is to add a fourth column to the K-W-L table (see Table 7.2), a column for what students still want to know. This S step promotes Information Age thinking in which students need to know where to find information. This fourth step also provides students with choice to pursue their own interests and then share what they learned with groupmates.

Problem-based learning

Problem-Based Learning (PBL), mentioned in Chapter 3, is a teaching method in which a problem actually drives the learning, and students discover that they need information or skill to solve a problem. PBL is student-centered, which problems are relevant to students serving as the organizing focus and catalyst for learning which usually occurs in small groups. The language teacher's function is to act as a facilitator of learning and to keep the students focused and on task and to encourage them to use all their language skills to inform other students. In second language learning the problems are a vehicle for learning the second language and for developing problem-solving skills and development of their second language skills (Neville & Britt, 2007). Second language learners develop a sense of self-directed learning a second language because they use that second language to learn how to

- organize prior knowledge about the problem
- discover the nature of the problem at hand
- pose relevant questions about the problem

- formulate a plan for solving the problem
- decide on proper resources to solve the problem
- generate possible solutions
- weigh the pros and cons of each possible solution
- select one solution
- test solution.

Practicing vigilance

While some textbooks and grammar books may attempt to present language as simple and straightforward, anyone who studies any language and who reflects on their own language use and the use of those in their environment will readily agree with the eminent linguist, Michael Halliday who once stated in a talk in Singapore that language is more complicated than nuclear physics. Although this complexity makes learning a second language, and even a first language, more difficult, it also opens up myriad opportunities for students to develop and employ their Thinking Skills as they grapple to understand the ever-changing ways that human language operates. The following story illustrates language's complexity.

A teacher, Ketsara Kumpoomprasert, observed a junior colleague teaching a lesson that focused on one of the differences between "can" and "could."

"Can you swim?" she asked one student, who replied, "Yes, I can."

"Could you swim when you were two years old?" she then asked, and he replied, "No, I could not."

This was exactly what the teacher had hoped to hear, and she used this real life example to tell the class, "He can swim now, but he could not swim when he was two years old."

The teacher continued to lead the class to develop more examples, which they did fairly successfully. Thus, it was with a feeling of accomplishment that the teacher ended the class and collected the instruments of her trade in preparation for moving on to her next class. As the teacher's arms were full, she asked the same student to help her with the door.

"Could you open the door for me?"

After a little thought, the student smiled and replied, "No, I couldn't but I can now because I've already finished my exercise."

Role of teachers

ESL teachers should resist the temptation to think that teaching Thinking Skills is the role of content area teachers, and that our job is only to provide students with the language skills they need for thinking. We ESL teachers do indeed have very important roles within a CLT approach to play to encourage our students to think critically and creatively. For example, we must show how to use such Thinking Skills as recognizing main ideas when they read and then formulating and highlighting main ideas in their own writing. We can scaffold for thinking in many ways, for example, by,

- providing clear models
- demonstrating
- helping students choose topics about which they have the background knowledge need for thinking tasks
- providing graphic organizers and other tools that promote thinking
- facilitating student–student interaction in setting where risk taking is promoted
- teaching students questions to use to encourage themselves and peers to think more deeply, such as questions from a variety of categories in Bloom's Taxonomy.

Role of students

For Thinking Skills to work with students they must become curious consumers of knowledge and not believe what they see or hear or read on first take. This means that they must be able to go beyond their comfort zones and develop a tolerance for ambiguity in that they may not know all the answers (incidentally their teachers must also be able to develop such a tolerance for ambiguity), nor even the correct questions; however, they will also discover over time that they will develop the courage to ask questions and thus may ultimately become producers of knowledge rather than just consumers of other people's ideas. Surely this is the whole point in educating our children.

Conclusion

The amount of knowledge is increasing in geometric proportions in our world. Perhaps at one time, it was possible to know most of what there was to know. Now that is clearly impossible. Rather than knowing every fact, we need to know how to find, evaluate, and synthesize facts. This chapter on Thinking

Skills has outlined the importance of this concept within a CLT approach to second language education and how teachers can implement such an approach in their ESL classes. This essential aspect of CLT maintains as our ESL students become critical thinkers; they can move from a position where they have been consumers of others' knowledge to a position where they can become creators of knowledge for others and thus be productive members of our society.

Reflections

- What is your understanding of Thinking Skills?
- Have you ever tried to show your ESL students how Thinking Skills in English are used throughout their studies in school?
- If yes, how did you go about this and were you successful?
- If no, how do you think you would go about this?
- What do you think of Mrs. Haley's method of teaching cause-and-effect?
- Would you teach it in any different way? If yes, how?
- What do you know about Bloom's Taxonomy and have you ever used it? If yes to using it, how did you use it?
- How do you teach writing? What does critical writing mean to you?
- How do you teach reading? What does critical reading mean to you?
- What is your opinion of the *SUMMER* activity and how would you adapt it to your context?

Utilize Alternative Assessment Methods 8

Vignette

John Smith was grading papers one day when he wondered what exactly his middle school ESL students were learning. John usually assessed his students using traditional testing methods of multiple-choice type tests and essay writing because he found that this way of testing the students yielded specific results that to some degree helped him reflect what his students knew at different times during the semester. These were in addition to the standardized test that students took in his school at the end of the year. However, John also realizes that each one of his students is unique and has different skills and abilities that are not always reflected in the results of these tests. For example, John knows that Mary, who is shy and exam phobic, is excellent at project work and assignment organization, and realizes that she should be assessed in a way that would fairly reflect these abilities. So, John, while not abandoning the traditional methods of assessment for his class as a whole, has decided to add a portfolio assessment approach for his writing class. He set this up by telling his students that these portfolios would contain a record of all their work and their progress during the year in their writing such as all the drafts of their writing, from the very first rough draft to the final version of the essay. John and other teachers in the school decided on general criteria that they would use for grading these portfolios and they also asked the students to help establish these criteria. For example, all students agreed that John would review these portfolios once a month and that students would be assessed based on how they updated their portfolios and their reflections on their own writing development. After using this Alternative Assessment method for his writing class, John has noticed that students like Mary are much more productive and seem to enjoy writing class more. This progress may be a direct result of being able to see the different drafts that each essay has gone through. More importantly, Mary (and other students) no longer fears assessment and her grade better reflects her work holistically.

Of course, we language teachers cannot escape from doing assessment, as it is essential for us to evaluate how effective our teaching is, and assessment serves as a guide to how we will plan future lessons. Traditional assessment formats, such as multiple-choice tests, matching, true–false, fill-in-the-blanks, short-answer, and essay, are the norms in many language classrooms and should not be discounted, because they provide language teachers and students with some indication of progress. *Multiple-choice* tests offer the test-takers a choice of choosing the correct answer out of a number of choices, *short-answer item* tests require students to supply a word, or a sentence in response to a question or a statement that they must complete, while the traditional *essay item* tests, the most common form of assessment, are when teachers want students to generate long answers in the form of a paragraph or a complete essay (usually consisting of 3–5 paragraphs).

Language teachers have long used such assessment devices, and we suggest that they continue to do so; however, we suggest that the essential of Alternative Assessment can also be used as an option for language teachers because these Alternative Assessments are ongoing, formative measures rather than one-time, summative test results (that discriminate against a student like Mary in the opening vignette of this chapter). This chapter outlines and discusses the essential of Alternative Assessment within a CLT approach to second language education.

Alternative assessment

Many teachers will tell you that they are required to test or assess their students these days more than at any other time in the past. Assessment involves the "documentation of student performance that is planned, collected, and interpreted by language teachers as part of the instructional cycle" (Gottlieb, 2006, p. 8). Just as the contents of all the previous chapters have suggested that the overall CLT approach has expanded expectations for what second language students need to learn to include such areas as fluency and not just accuracy, social appropriacy of use, and Thinking Skills, we maintain that the CLT approach has also advanced alternative means of assessing student language learning that complement rather than replace traditional instruments that use multiple choice, true–false, and fill-in-the-blank items and that focus on accuracy, grammar, and lower-order thinking.

Alternative Assessment instruments attempt to more closely mirror real-life conditions and involve higher order Thinking Skills. Although these instruments are often more time-consuming for teachers to implement, as well as more difficult to use in a reliable manner in terms of consistency of scoring, they are gaining prominence due to dissatisfaction with traditional modes of assessment, which are faulted for not capturing vital information about students' competence in their second language and for only serving to measure students, not to teach them. Even when students have to take large-scale standardized tests, Alternative Assessment can help them prepare for these (Stiggins, 2007) because the goal of Alternative Assessment is not just assessing; the goal is also to teach. With these Alternative Assessment methods at our disposal, language teachers can now include five important features of assessment not included in traditional testing:

- First, there is an emphasis placed on *meaning* rather than form. This emphasis underlies many of the new assessment instruments outlined in this chapter.
- Second, many of the Alternative Assessment methods outlined in this chapter seek to investigate process rather than end product.
- Third, the understanding of the Social Nature of Learning has led to the inclusion of peer assessment and to the use of group tasks in Alternative Assessments.
- Fourth, in keeping with notions of Learner Autonomy, students are now more involved in their own learning processes and how these processes will be assessed, understanding how they will be assessed, and even participating in that assessment. For example, self-assessment can be an important part of Alternative Assessment.
- Fifth, linking Alternative Assessment to integrated curriculum, students are now asked to engage in assessment tasks that have a real world feel thus integrating with the world beyond the classroom.

Figure 8.1, below, outlines some of the main differences between Alternative Assessment and traditional assessment.

Alternative Assessment	Traditional Assessment
• Represents a complete range of topics and subjects students are engaged in	• Assesses students across a limited range of topics and subjects
• Cannot be mechanically scored. Often some form of scoring rubric is used	• Can often be mechanically scored or scored by teachers using an answer key
• Students are involved in their assessment.	• Scoring is done exclusively by the teacher or a machine
• Assessment is collaborative: teacher and students	• Assessment not collaborative
• Student peer- and self-assessment ultimate goal	• No student peer- or self-assessment
• Allows for individual differences in achievement	• Assesses all students on the same criterion
• Assessment for achievement and development—effort included	

Figure 8.1 Alternative assessment versus traditional assessment

Classroom implications

Portfolios

Portfolios are a systematic collection of information about each student. This information consists of evidence of students' accomplishments and skills. Students are responsible for compiling their own portfolio and, it must be updated as the students develop and add to their achievements. Most importantly, portfolios encourage students to take more responsibility and ownership for their own learning. Gottlieb (2006) suggests that portfolios are excellent ways for students to showcase their newly acquired language skills as well as to share their accomplishments. Another means of sharing involves supplementing portfolios with one-on-one conferences with the teacher or peer conferencing. Construction and assessment of portfolios is facilitated when teachers and students have come to joint decisions regarding the *content, quantity, quality, timing,* and *presentation* of portfolio entries before the process begins. Of course, these decisions can be modified, as a class becomes more familiar with the portfolio process.

In a writing course, using the example of the change in approach to teaching and learning writing, portfolios offer language teachers a complimentary means of looking at students' writing processes (Rea, 2001). With portfolio assessment, students keep the writing they have done over the course of a term or more, including early drafts. Then, they analyze their writing to understand the progress they have made. Next, they select from among their pieces of writing to compile a collection that demonstrates the path of their writing journey. To promote student reflection on their learning journey, students also prepare an introduction to the portfolio in which they present their findings as to what they have learned, how they have learned it, their strengths and weaknesses, and what they can do to continue toward becoming full-fledged members of the community of writers in their target language.

Devising a scoring system for portfolios requires careful thought, because some scoring guides can be so detailed that evaluators can become overwhelmed, while other guides may be too general as to render the scoring process too subjective. The key is to come up with a balanced scoring system. Although the contents of student portfolios may vary greatly, guidance sheets for their students that can suggest a familiar structure to each portfolio entry, for example:

- *Description*: What is this entry?
- *Reason*: Why did I include this entry?
- *Opinion*: Why do I think this entry is important? What am I proud of in this entry?
- *Reflection*: What did I accomplish with this entry?
- *Teacher comments* (optional): Teachers (and peers) can add comments after each entry.

Peer assessment

Another alternative form of assessment in education involves peers, where students themselves evaluate each other's levels of participation, work samples, and behavior in the class. Students can rate their peers in many ways. For example, students can use the same rating instruments as teachers use such as when students give a presentation in class, their peers can fill in the same rating scale that the teacher uses, either along with the teacher or instead of the teacher. To make the task easier for students, they might only use some of the items that teachers use, or the items might be divided among students, so that each student or group of students focus on just one item, e.g., in assessing speaking, some students might focus on whether a peer spoke with the proper degree of loudness, while others listen for fluency. Instead of using an instrument developed by the teacher or taken from an established text, the students can design their own rating instruments with the guidance of their teacher. Also, they can rate their peers on matters that teachers may know less about, such as students' participation in their group. Regardless of how the peer assessment instrument is developed and what the instrument looks at, time should probably be spent to help students understand the instrument and how to use it. When properly conducted, peer assessment adds a new dimension to assessment and may make assessment seem more equitable in the students' eyes. Examples of peer assessment items include:

- Who are some of the hardest workers in class?
- Who are some of the people who work the least in class?
- Which student(s) helps his/her fellow students the most with homework/classwork?
- Which student(s) helps his/her fellow students the least with homework/classwork?
- Which student(s) shares materials with his/her fellow students the most?
- Which student(s) shares materials with his/her fellow students the least?
- Which student(s) does his/her homework the best?
- Which student(s) seldom does his/her homework?

- Which student(s) does not do well on tests but works hard?
- Were tenses used properly in your groupmate's essay?

From these data, teachers can obtain extra information about their students; information about the students from the students. Teachers must be careful to realize however, that some of the students' answers about their peers may have an element of assessing their peers' social acceptance rather than an honest answer. Therefore, teachers should carefully explain the reason for using this rating system to their students before they use it.

In addition to providing an alternative source of assessment data, peer feedback offers another important advantage. When students attend to particular features of their peers' work, this focus helps students attend to and understand features that teachers and students have agreed are valuable. The hope is that, as a result of peer assessment, students will focus on these same features in their own work, thereby enhancing the quality of that work. Here is an example of an area in which the experience of doing peer assessment might subsequently improve individuals' own efforts. Many students have difficulty with reference when they speak and write. For instance, they use multiple pronouns without careful attention to what or whom the pronouns refer, e.g., "My brother loaned his friend his MP3 player, and his friend loaned him his game player, but then he broke it." If students are assigned to check the reference in peers' work, by focusing on this specific aspect, students grow their understanding of reference, and their awareness grows as well. Therefore, when students do their own writing, they may be more likely to exercise care regarding reference.

Although in the example above of the students' reference error, sometimes peer assessment will highlight errors, it may actually be more useful to focus peer assessment on what peers have done well. Indeed, a frequent teacher-induced assessment error that students make is focusing on the negative in the mistaken view that good assessment is mostly about hunting for errors (Compton, 2005). We call this a teacher-induced error because in too many cases, students have been endured a steady diet of teacher assessment which included seeing their assignments and tests returned to them bloodied by their teachers' red pens.

If in contrast, students (not to mention teachers) focus their feedback on what peers have done well, it builds students' confidence that they can indeed communicate successfully in the target language. However, it must be stressed that this positive feedback is not just a stream of vague expressions of praise, such as "Good job!" and "Awesome!" Positive assessments should be specific (Chalk & Bizo, 2004). They must say and show what exactly peers have done well. Such specificity is both for the sake of students receiving the praise, as well as for those giving the praise, not to mention those third parties, e.g., the third and fourth members of a group of four, who witness the specific praise. An example of showing would be, to return to the learning of reference, students circling the pronouns and the nouns to which they refer in a peer's writing, and then drawing lines to connect pronouns to the appropriate nouns.

Self-reports

Self-reports are student self-generated documentation of how they think they are progressing and promote direct involvement in the learning process. Gottlieb (2006) suggests that self-reports benefit students in the following ways; they

- provide a venue for students to convey their depth of understanding
- invite students to take responsibility for their own learning
- honor student input in the assessment process
- recognize the student perspective as a valid data source
- foster the creation of a shared set of expectations between teachers and students
- encourage students to do their best work
- help students set realistic goals based on their accomplishments
- offer personalized feedback to teachers
- promote students becoming life time learners.

Self-reports are most important because they involve students directly in the assessment process thus providing them greater motivation to learn. They are also a useful way of obtaining information directly from the students. In addition, language teachers would have a better sense of what their language students are able to do if only they would ask them for example, to summarize what they have done (by drawing, speaking, or writing), describe their favorite or most challenging activity, or explain some aspect of learning of the language. Gottlieb (2006) outlines the following *Biography Self-Assessment* that has students list what they accomplished during their assignment as follows:

- Write a list of persons who you admire and respect. Then chose a person to study.
- Collect information on the person from two sources (books, the Internet, newspapers, magazines).

- Include: personal information; important life events; contributions to society.
- Make a chart of the similarities and differences in what the two sources say about the person.
- Summarize the information from the two sources.
- Find pictures or other visuals about the life of the person.
- Use all the above information to write a 1- to 2-page biography with pictures.

As with peer assessments, self-reports need to highlight what students have done well and the progress they have made, in preparation for further progress ahead. Such a positive outlook may enhance students' self concept. Self concept is people's perception of themselves. It is learned over time, beginning from an early age, as a result of verbal and nonverbal reactions of significant others – parents, teachers, siblings, peers, and the individuals themselves. Self concept can be general, as well as specific to particular contexts. Self concept forms the basis for students' assessments of themselves as language learners and their predictions as to their ultimate level of language attainment. Too many students have formed negative self concepts of themselves as language learners and users. Too many brilliant lesson plans have been sunk by students unwilling to believe that they have the capability to succeed at the tasks in the lesson.

Anecdotal records

Teachers know their individual students better than anybody else and especially in terms of their linguistic abilities, their willingness to participate in class, how they take tests and how they generally prefer to learn a second language. This knowledge is built up from the teachers' daily observations of their students in action in their classrooms (and outside the classrooms). Gottlieb (2006) suggests that structured observation, where teachers systematically maintain written anecdotal records of their students over time, can be used successfully to focus on specific aspects of their students' literacy development and systematically document their performance over time.

Attitude scales

Alternative Assessment involves not just the assessment of students but also the assessment of teachers, the curriculum, and other factor that impact students' experience in education. Attitudes scales provide one means of collecting data on such topics. These scales, usually designed by teachers, can be a useful means of gauging the students' feelings and opinions about various aspects of their schooling such as *classroom activities, peers, school events, teachers, and administrators*. These scales can give teachers a more detailed understanding of their students' preferences for certain activities and the like and can aid teachers with their planning, both inside and outside the classroom. For example, regarding classroom activities, teachers can design an attitude scale for activities conducted in specific subject matter areas such as in a Math class taught in the second language. Teachers can design a scale that measures their students' liking for such activities as adding, problem solving, playing math games, and doing math homework. Teachers can obtain useful information from these scales about their students' perceptions of certain activities that can be used for teacher lesson planning and course revisions. However, teachers should also realize that sometimes students may perceive an activity that they cannot do or feel negatively about regardless of how educational, important, or useful the activity may be. Because teachers are the people closest to their students, they are the best to judge the value of the overall responses.

Alternative testing of language proficiency skills

Regarding testing discrete skills of proficiency in a language, Alternative Assessment has much to offer language teachers. For example, Gottlieb (2006) suggests that English language learners may demonstrate their listening comprehension skills in nonverbal ways such as simply pointing to the objects in an illustrated book in response to questions or commands in a listening test. In addition, a two-way task can add the oral dimension in assessment where each of paired English language learners has half the information on a graphic, such as location of places or landmarks on a map, and through commands or phrases, attempts to complete the missing half with the partner. In addition to the above, Gottlieb (2006) suggests that language teachers interested in alternative modes of language assessment consider the following activities (used individually or in combination):

- Debates on school-related topics or current issues
- Dialogues between students on social or culturally related topics
- Interviews between students or between students and adults
- Presentations/reports on content-related assignments
- Role plays/dramatizations of historical or social events
- Speeches or reports based on research or topics of interest

- Task analyses or demonstrations on how to do activities, processes, or procedures
- Story (re)telling from illustrations or personal experiences
- Student-led conferences on original work or portfolios
- The use of visuals, such as drawings, mindmaps, and flow charts (all of which computer software facilitates)
- Poems that represent concepts and information learned
- Songs that put those concepts and that information into words and use familiar tunes

Group tests

In keeping with the essential of the Social Nature of Learning (Chapter 3), some teachers are using group tests as an alternative to or as a preparation for the more traditional individual tests. For example, Hicks (2007) used group tests with radiologic technology students. His rationale was quite similar to one of those expressed in Chapter 3: students need to know how to communicate and cooperate in the work world, and group tests serve to prepare students for that. Hicks found that after completing the course, students' acceptance of group tests increased. Similarly, group projects, such as Problem-Based Learning (Lambros, 2004) are often done instead of individual ones.

Practicing vigilance

A frequent problem in assessment stems from lack of common expectations between students and teachers as to the goal, i.e., what is being assessed. This edited story, told originally by Peter Brown, illustrates such as mismatch between a father, who can't stop being an English teacher, and his 5-year-old son. The boy thinks the goal of the discussion is to relate with what happened at school, whereas the father's focus seems interested only in the boy's grammar. The story begins with the boy recounting what happened at a jumble sale at his school the previous day.

> *Boy:* My friend Robin didn't have enough money, so I gived him one of my coins and then he bought a cake and then I gived the man another coin too for a cake.
> *Father:* You shouldn't say, "I buyed a cake." You should say, "I …"
> *Boy:* "Bought."
> *Father:* So why did you say, "Buyed?"
> *Boy:* I don't know. Let's switch it off!
> *Father:* Well, alright then . . . and what did you do with the cake you bought?

Boy: I eated it all.
Father: You said, "I eated." What should you say?
Boy: "Ate."
Father: Well, why did you say, "Eated"?
Boy: Well, er … I don't Knoooooooooooooooow!
Father: Oh, alright! … How about if I hop around like a kangaroo every time you say "eated" and "buyed"? (the father begins to hop)
Boy: Stop!
Father: Alright.

Role of teachers

Second language teachers have the following vitally important roles to play when designing Alternative Assessments as follows:

- *Teachers understand learning processes*. Teachers must realize that learning a second language is not a linear process and that students need to be encouraged along the way with examples of progress from specific evidence from their own work such as in portfolio examples. This again shows them that learning is a process; it is not, as is emphasized in many traditional tests, only a product. Students can become more involved in their own processes of learning.
- *Teachers as models of Alternative Assessment*. In this chapter we suggested that the new paradigm approach to teaching and learning writing involves writing as a process.from brainstorming at the beginning to the first draft, to other multiple drafts to the final draft. Teachers too can show their students their own writing drafts and explain how writing is also a process of discovery for them rather than producing a perfect end product. Both students and teachers can engage in a discussion of their learning processes (see Chapter 9 on Teachers as Co-learners) and students can then try to apply some of the strategies they may have picked up from these conversations in their own learning.
- *Teachers as developers of different assessments*. Language teachers will be most active in designing and implementing these alternative methods of assessment because all we really have now is the ready-made traditional tests and many of these commercially produced. Of course, as we will see in the next section, students will also be asked to contribute to the design and implementation of Alternative Assessments.

Role of students

Teachers need not design Alternative Assessment tasks alone. For example, when designing assessments that take real-life situations into consideration, teachers need to consider what people do in their everyday jobs. In order to learn about this, teachers can involve students by asking them to interview people in various careers. In this way, students can begin to see relationships between the real world and what they learn in school. The students can see exactly why they are doing the particular assignments. The students can ask these people to answer such questions as follow:

- What do professors study in their daily work? How do they do it?
- How do newspaper writers get their ideas?
- How do scientists identify, study, and solve problems?
- How do restaurant managers organize different aspects of their work?

Students can be further involved by having them set the criteria by which their assignments will be assessed. These criteria should be agreed upon before the start of the assignment so that each student (and the teacher) is aware of what is required. Students are also involved in the peer and self assessment components of Alternative Assessment.

Conclusion

This chapter has outlined Alternative Assessment methods. It showed that new assessment instruments have been developed to complement (or even replace) traditional instruments that use multiple choice, true–false, and fill-in-the-blank items and that mostly tend to focus on lower-order thinking (Stiggins, 2007; Wiggins, 1998) and a process–product approach to learning. Alternative Assessment instruments, on the other hand, attempt to more closely mirror real-life conditions where people struggle though process while arriving at product. Thus, assessment captures vital information about students' development through the process of learning. Although these instruments are often more time-consuming and costly to use, as well as less reliable in terms of consistency of scoring, they are gaining prominence due to dissatisfaction with traditional modes of assessment, which are faulted for not capturing vital information about students' competence in their second language. Now, even when students have to take large-scale standardized tests, Alternative Assessment can help them prepare for these (Wiggins, 1998) because the goal of Alternative Assessment is not just assessing; the goal is also to teach. In fact, students who are assessed with Alternative Assessment instruments may even be better prepared to take standardized tests because they are more aware of learning as a process of discovery and that a standardized test is only one measure of that learning.

Reflections

- Reread the anecdote at the beginning of this chapter. Do you think John Smith is a typical language teacher in terms of his reflection on his students' need for Alternative Assessment? If yes, why? If not, why not?
- How do you approach the whole idea of testing and assessment? Is there a difference for you between assessment and testing and if so, what is the difference?
- What is your understanding of Alternative Assessment?
- List some of the advantages and disadvantages of Alternative Assessment.
- What criteria do you think should be part of the evaluation process of a portfolio in order to make scoring consistent?
- Can you think of any other means of assessing second language students?

Promote English Language Teachers as Co-learners

Chapter Outline

Vignette

Lucille Michaels teaches Spanish at her high school. For a recent 12th grade class, the main course objective was for the students to be able to write a full essay at the end of the course. When thinking about how to teach the course Lucille wondered if before each assigned essay she should lecture about how to write, give them a model essay and then ask her students to work on an essay similar to the model one so that she could monitor and control their writing. Alternatively, she wondered if she should let each student work alone on their own essay based on their individual interests. Lucille, as a believer in learner-centeredness and in trying to make learning meaningful to students, decided to encourage students to come up with their own essay topics (based on their individual purposes for writing and the audiences they chose to write for), and work together in groups of two or three to share their work with the other students so that her students could get a sense of audience for their writing. Lucille was pleasantly surprised during the term and especially at the end of the semester, for not only had students completed their own essays, but she herself had learned a lot from all the different topics they had written about, and Lucille felt she knew her students better as people from the interaction she had with them and from observing their interaction with peers. She also learned more about her students' writing processes and how to facilitate them. Part of this pedagogic learning came from what she had listened to in the group discussions because of the many diverse questions students asked each other when writing drafts of their essays, the problems they encountered when writing their drafts, and the solutions they all came up with together in their groups.

Some teachers and administrators perceive their students as receivers of their knowledge and believe that the best way they can learn is by following teachers' directions in a "chalk-and-talk" style learning environment. However, this chapter outlines and discusses the idea that teachers and students actually become co-learners in the second language classroom. This essential of Teachers as Co-learners within a CLT approach to second language education involves teachers learning along with students.

Teachers as co-learners

The essential of Teachers as Co-learners focuses on second language education teachers learning *along with* the students (and teacher colleagues), learning *from* the students while at the same time learning *about* the students such as their first language education backgrounds, their lives and learning various teaching methods from colleagues. Because the world is complex and constantly changing, life-long learning is available and is important for both teachers and their students. Teachers, by their very choice of profession, have expressed an unquenchable delight in learning and, indeed, model this desire for their students so that they too can catch the same life-long thrill of learning and sharing one's learning. In this learning process, teachers learn more about their subject, in this case the second language they are teaching, and they learn more about their students and about people generally. They also learn more about how to teach (Bailey & Nunan, 1996; Freeman & Richards, 1996). To promote their learning, teachers depend more on themselves, their colleagues and their students, rather than on outside experts. This is sometimes called bottom-up professional development (Richards & Farrell, 2005).

In many institutions and language schools, second language teachers are seen as workers who need to be supervised by so-called "experts," and usually from the university and relevant government ministries and other such institutions, in order to make sure that prescribed curriculum goals are being met and students are performing according to these predetermined schemes such as learning x number of new vocabulary words each week, or learning the past tense verbs within a two-week lesson period (outcomes of which include being able to fill in the blanks of the correct verb tense in decontexualized sentences). Within this view (some would say the "old paradigm" view) of language education, teaching is seen as a skill that can be learned in discrete items from how to plan lessons to how to ask questions in class. When these skills have been learned, the teacher is seen as qualified to teach. In second language teacher education this approach is seen as "training" (Freeman, 1989). In the previous paradigm, second language teachers' opinions and experiences are more often than not excluded. Instead, the "experts" in the universities do the research on how to teach and administrators do the assessment of teaching effectiveness. Their pronouncements are then handed down to practitioners. However, the eight *essentials* view of second language education as discussed in this book sees teaching and learning as social processes where the students are active co-constructors of knowledge with their teachers. The teachers are more of facilitators and fellow learners alongside the students and who are responsible for not just the students learning, but also their own as well as that of their colleagues.

In fact, the theory behind how teachers learn parallels that behind how students learn. In other words, the same theories which argue the other seven essentials discussed in these pages' seven previous chapters, apply to teachers just as they do to students. In the traditional paradigm, top-down decision making and external control by experts from universities and government agencies is emphasized as the most efficient way to promote education. As the Minister of Education of one country once boasted to a visitor, "It's 10:00am. I can tell you what page in their textbook every teacher in the country is on right now." Teachers have a rigid set of content, materials, and methods to follow and are to follow that without exception in order to ensure uniformity and prepare students for standardized exams. However, with an Essentials view to language education, a more bottom-up decision making process is used by both teachers and their students. Language teachers are considered (and appreciated) as full-fledged professionals who, individually and collaboratively, do their own thinking and conduct their own research so that they can learn how to best cater to the particular needs of their own language students. As such, language Teachers as Co-learners take more responsibility for curriculum development and implementation so that their students can have language learning experiences adapted to their specific needs. Also, when teachers see the effectiveness and experience the joy of learning in this way, they desire deeply to facilitate similar success and similar experiences for their students.

Classroom implications

Teachers and students learning together

Second language teachers have many ways to create an environment in which students come to see their teachers not as all-knowing second language experts infallibly dispensing knowledge, but as fellow searchers after learning. This may sound strange to those students who depend on the language teachers as a source of input for language practice but consider the following ways teachers can learn together with their students:

- Asking students about their experiences, knowledge, and opinions on the topics being written and talked about during second language practice and also share your own.
- Asking students to do research on specific topics and then report on their findings to the class so that all can learn not only the second language in question but also some new information for the teacher and the other students. Teachers can also do research.
- Admitting to students when we make errors or do not know something about the target language we teach, regardless of what students expect. And, we explore with students how to use various resources to check our ideas and to learn new information about the language.
- Talking about our own history as second language learners, either of the target language or of another language.
- If we are in the beginning or intermediate stages of learning a language that one or more of our students speak, we might every once in a while use that language with students as a way to show that we are willing to risk stepping outside our language comfort zone.

- Expressing wonder at the marvelous and endless complexities of language. Paraphrasing a remark once made by noted linguist Michael Halliday at a lecture, "Language is much more complicated than nuclear physics."
- Inviting students to take part in choosing topics of study in order to promote students' interest in learning and to make it more likely students will possess background knowledge on those topics rather than selecting the same topic for each student to talk and/or write about which is (unfortunately) common practice in many schools today.
- Be willing to let the entire class discover learning as they go along. In fact, language teachers do not need to fully structure their daily lesson plans to the point that each class minute is planned.
- Be willing to jettison the lesson plan to talk about something in today's headlines or something which has just happened in the school or elsewhere in students' lives.
- Inviting students to teach others about what they learned, thus increasing their feelings of expertise.
- Communicating our enthusiasm for the topic the class is studying by sharing our experiences, thoughts, and opinions as equal contributors to the learning moment.
- Participating alongside students in their activities, and not standing off watching and listening "like a teacher" that is the case in many classrooms. For example, while students do independent reading, teachers also read. Then, when students share about what they've read, teachers do too. Even if teachers have read something beyond students in terms of language level and/or cognitive complexity, teachers can share in a way that students can understand.

However, just because teachers are no longer in total control (or omniscient sages on stages) does not mean that they are just like any other class member with no special knowledge, skills, or role. It's a bit like realizing that we are experts in certain areas, and students are experts in others. By sharing our expertise and welcoming the expertise of others, we all learn more and the classroom becomes a more equitable, livelier place to be.

Teacher mentoring

Second language teachers can implement teacher as co-learner by engaging in some form of reflective practice with their students, where beliefs and practices are subjected to some scrutiny (Farrell, 2007). For this to happen, both teachers and their students should reflect on their teaching and learning. For example, teachers help each other learn when more experienced or more effective teachers serve as mentors for peers. Research has indicated that beginning teachers who are mentored are more effective teachers in their early years and are more likely to remain in teaching, since they learn from guided practice rather than depending upon trial-and-error alone (Porter, 2008). The mentor–mentee relationship need not be one in which a gap exists between the two in terms of experience. Two teachers at the same experience level and same rank in the teaching hierarchy can form a critical friendship. A critical friend acts as an observer who can talk about teaching in a collaborative undertaking and give advice as a friend, in order to develop the reflective abilities of the teacher who is conducting his/her own action research (Yeigh, 2008).

Peer coaching

Peer coaching also emphasizes collegiality between colleagues because one teacher will learn from a colleague (Bruce & Ross, 2008). Teachers become empowered to set their own goals, by analyzing their teaching with the help of a peer. The peer, acting as coach/friend, offers suggestions to a colleague based on classroom observations. Teachers make their own decisions as to what changes, if any, to incorporate into their teaching. In other words, each teacher still has the main responsibility to develop and does not hand over control to a colleague. Suggestions as to how teachers can act as coaches to foster language teacher development include the following:

- Informal chats about their teaching in the form of anecdotes about what is happening in their classroom.
- Collaborating to design materials.
- If colleagues are teaching the same subject area, they can come together and analyze what they are doing and make suggestions to add or take out some of the existing curriculum.
- Observing each other's lessons.
- Co-teaching lessons and observing each other's approach and teaching style.
- Video taping lessons and watching them together.

An example of this can happen when the *coach* observes the fellow teacher and makes a record of the observation. Depending on the amount of detail required by the teacher and the focus of the observation, which is decided by the teacher (not the coach), both will reflect on practice. Remember, the main purpose of peer coaching is to support a teacher's existing strengths and develop unexplored capacities. The process has three main phases: Pre-observation meeting; classroom observation; post-observation meeting. The classroom observation may be assisted by the following data-gathering instruments: audio-tape; video-tape; classroom transcriptions. Both parties may reflect on the whole process by engaging in journal writing and discussions. Both participants should write down their reflections of the process and what was achieved. They should then meet and discuss what was written and what was achieved.

Teachers conducting research

One way for teachers (and students) to learn more is by doing research, rather than relying solely on the research of others from outside the classroom. For example, Freeman (1996) suggests that it is necessary to "put the person who does the work at the center" (p. 90) of that work and the best way to do this is to have practicing teachers research their own classrooms. His basic premise for putting teachers at the center follows a jazz maxim: "you have to know the story in order to tell the story" (p. 89). So, language teachers have the inside view of their world in that they live in it each day and know up close what issues are most important for them and their students. There has been some heated discussion however in second language education circles about what constitutes real research and how this should be conducted by practicing language teachers. Sometimes this argument comes down to two main approaches to research and data collection, namely, quantitative, the more traditional approach that includes large scale data collection and a lot of number crunching at the end, and the newer qualitative approach that allows for an insider's view of what is happening (and in our opinion more appropriate for language teachers conducting classroom research).

One form that teacher research can take is action research in which teachers – alone, with colleagues, with students, and/or with outsiders – conduct small-scale research to address questions or concerns that have arisen in their teaching (Richards & Farrell, 2005). Teachers then share this research with others, thus establishing a source of knowledge on teaching that is organic to the school. Action research concerns research into action and through action. At the heart of action research is the idea that language teachers must take some action to improve their practice. In order to carry out an action research project, teachers can follow several steps to make this possible:

Step 1 – A problem, issue, question
- o Problem: Students are too noisy when they work in groups
- o Question: How to integrate Thinking Skills, extensive reading?
- o Issue: Intrinsic vs extrinsic motivation in extensive reading

Step 2 – Search for information
- o books
- o journals
- o internet
- o colleagues
- o the person next to us on the bus
- o parents
- o students

Step 3 – Make an action plan
- o To reduce noise during group work, students sit closer together and use 30 cm voices (voices that can only be heard 30 cm away)
- o To integrate Thinking Skills, we explain what thinking questions are; students write their own for peers to answer
- o To investigate different means of motivating students, we do one series of classes with intrinsic motivators and another series with extrinsic

Step 4 – Collect baseline data
- o Audio and/or video record the class
- o Estimate noise level on a 10-point scale
- o Examine students' answers to higher-order questions for evidence of thinking
- o Estimate level of students' motivation by observing how frequently students are on-task or by asking students via interview or questionnaire

Step 5 – Implement your plan
- o Involve colleagues and others

Step 6 – Collect more data

Step 7 – Analyze your data
- o Compare with baseline
- o Ask why changes or lack thereof
- o Add own intuition

Step 8 – Share your findings
- o Staff sharing session
- o Internet discussion groups with other language teachers
- o Other language schools
- o Journals/magazines/newspapers
- o Students
- o Parents, Community
- o Administrators
- o Education conferences

Step 9 – Make a new plan
- Can be follow-up to previous one
  - o Can involve new people (new class, new teachers, new content area)

o Can take up a related question, issue, or problem
o Or can involve a new topic
- Research often raises more questions than it answers.

Role of teachers

Teachers have the following vitally important roles to play when seeking a co-learning relationship within the eight essentials as follows:

- ***Teachers as searchers for knowledge***. Teachers demonstrate to students that learning is a life-long pursuit. Learning is a messy business filled with ambiguity, uncertainty, false understandings, and overthrown beliefs. Nonetheless, it is an exhilarating journey, a journey as worthwhile as the destination.
- ***Teachers as models of effective learners***. Because teachers are learning along with students, they are in a position to act as models (of course they will also be obvious models of the second language they are teaching) by showing the students problem-solving strategies in whole-group activities and with smaller groups. The students then observe how these tasks are done and then asked to apply what they have learned (the strategies) in an observe–reflect–discuss–apply pattern.
- ***Teachers as guides***. We have a responsibility to act not only as co-explorers, but also as guides on the hike. As important as it is that we involve students in the curriculum, it is also important that we fulfill our roles as teachers – as those who have gone ahead, those who have experienced more, to guide students toward those experiences which we believe will be most educative; not just for that moment, but for the times that students cannot know what they might encounter.
- ***Teachers as researchers, materials developers, and decision makers***. Because teachers are seen as the experts on the own teaching rather than as technicians carrying out the plans and instructions of others, teachers' roles in the school broaden. Instead of being consumers of others' research, materials, and decisions, they are doing and making their own, in collaboration with colleagues.
- ***Teachers have to go off the beaten path***. Thus, textbooks and other ready-made materials will not suffice. Instead, teachers and students contribute materials that they find and develop as part of their quest for knowledge. Also, the knowledge in textbooks is questioned by new information and insights that teachers and students gather and create.
- ***Teachers as engaged intellectuals***. We all realize that what happens in our classrooms is impacted in a major way by the world outside. However, too often we educators limit our actions to the confines of our classrooms or at most our schools, leaving the wider arena to the politicians. A countervailing trend is for teachers to work collectively with colleagues and with students to become "engaged intellectuals" (Kecskes, 2006). Issues addressed can relate to education, such as English Only ballot initiatives or other matters, such as animal welfare or environmental

issues. In this way, we demonstrate to students that when we talk about connecting education to the wider world and about engaged citizenship, we are practicing what we preach.

Role of students

Students also have a very important role in ensuring that the essential of Teachers as Co-learners becomes a reality in our language classrooms. For example, students need to adjust if teachers are to succeed in being co-learners. Students are involved in,

- accepting that teachers do not know everything, that teachers, regardless of how intelligent and learned they may be, are trying to learn too
- understanding that new knowledge is being created all the time, thus rendering today's understanding as obsolete
- joining with teachers as investigators, seeking a better grasp of the content area they are studying as well as of their own and the classmates' education process
- acting as sources of information and insight for teachers and classmates
- collaborating with teachers to put their new-found knowledge to the service of others.

Conclusion

This chapter has discussed Teachers as Co-learners, an eighth essential within a CLT approach to second language education. For this essential both teachers and students learn while carrying out their particular roles in the classroom, and thus the classroom is seen to be a center of inquiry for both teachers and their students. In fact, the essential of Teachers as Co-learners maintains that just as students take more control of their own learning, so too do teachers have more control over their own teaching and develop their own professional growth paths. This connects with all the other chapters already discussed in this book. For instance, Teachers as Co-learners embrace the *Social Nature of learning* (see Chapter 3) where the co-learning that teachers engage in involves collaboration with peers, students, and others. It also involves the essential of *Thinking Skills* (see Chapter 7) because the learning that teachers undertake involves many complexities and calls for a variety of Thinking Skills.

Teachers, like others outside of formal education, learn in a contextualized manner, and they learn best when studying areas important to their lives. Such learning encourages teachers to facilitate similar learning environments for their students, and this also includes the essential *Focus on Meaning* (see Chapter 5). Teachers as co-learners also includes the essential of integrated curriculum (see Chapter 4) because even though teachers may be comfortable to stick with their familiar subject-area textbook year after year, this essential (Curricular Integration) pushes them to learn about other subject areas and to put aside the textbook now and then to link with particularities of students' lives. Of course, as teachers learn about students' lives they also come to appreciate student Diversity (see Chapter 6) and the wonderful variety that exists among the students, not to mention their own uniqueness as teachers given that they have different teaching styles, interests, and strengths. Language teachers should explore this student Diversity in order to gain a greater understanding of the students' backgrounds as also to understand themselves as learners. Alternative Assessment (see Chapter 8) also provides many tools for teachers to learn about their teaching and, along with others, to conduct research on education. Finally, Teachers as Co-learners fits with the essential *Learner Autonomy* (see Chapter 2) because just as students take on a larger role in their own learning, so do teachers take greater control over their own teaching.

Reflections

- Do you think that teachers and students can learn together or is this too lofty a goal for CLT?
- How can we create a situation such that the best teachers spend more time in the classroom? Often teachers who demonstrate better than average skill, devotion, and understanding are "promoted" to roles in which they spend less and less time in the classroom?
- Are all teachers suitable to become mentor teachers?
- What are the main difficulties with a peer coaching relationship?
- How valid is teacher research?
- What about teachers who only want to teach and are not interested in being mentors, researchers, materials developers, etc.?
- Look at the teacher roles in the essential of Teachers as Co-learners; do you think these are all achievable? Can you add more?

10 English Language Education: The Essentials

As stated in the preface, this book is about how we teach English as a second language (ESL) and English as a foreign language (EFL) and how our second language students learn. Kurt Lewin's famous dictum, "There's nothing as practical as a good theory" (Lewin, 1951, p. 169) probably best sums up how we arranged the contents of this book. We think the ideas presented in this book represent a practical approach to teaching second language, yet all the activities are backed up solidly with clearly explained theories about where they came from.

We also readily acknowledge that we are not creating new theories at the expense of older theories; rather educators at this time are developing and applying what others have already done, building upon, not demolishing, these excellent theories and practices, because we recognize that we could not have developed these eight essentials without having stout shoulders to stand on. As Einstein put it (quoted in Zukav, 2001, p. 19),

> Creating a new theory is not like destroying an old barn and erecting a skyscraper in its place. It is rather like climbing a mountain, gaining new and wider views, discovering unexpected connections between our starting point and its rich environment. But the point from which we started out still exists and can be seen, although it appears smaller and forms a tiny part of our broad view gained by the mastery of the obstacles on our adventurous way up.

Table 10.1 Contrasts between positivism and post-positivism

Positivism	Post-positivism
Emphasis on parts and decontextualization	Emphasis on whole and contextualization
Emphasis on separation	Emphasis on integration
Emphasis on the general	Emphasis on the specific
Consideration only of objective and the quantifiable	Consideration also of subjective and the non-quantifiable
Reliance on experts and outsider knowledge – researcher as external	Consideration also of the "average" participant and insider knowledge – researcher as internal
Focus on control	Focus on understanding
Top-down	Bottom-up
Attempt to standardize	Appreciation of diversity
Focus on the product	Focus on the process as well

In addition, and as already pointed out in Chapter 1 of this book, we consider our Eight Essentials as a type of "paradigm shift" and when a paradigm shift takes place, we see things from a different perspective. Twentieth century paradigm shifts across a wide variety of fields can be seen as part of a larger shift from positivism to post-positivism (Wheatley, 2006). Awareness of this broader shift helps make clearer the shifts that have taken place in second language education. Table 10.1 provides a brief look at some contrasts between positivism and post-positivism.

In second language education, the CLT paradigm shift, which started in the early 1970s, has become the driving force that affects the planning, implementation, and evaluation of many second language programs throughout the world, and as we suggested in Chapter 1, involves a move toward more inclusiveness in all areas of language learning and teaching. This means that both second language teachers and learners take on new roles in the classroom. Now, instead of mastering discrete grammar items through drill and memorization following a teacher model, learners take center stage as they interact with their peers, while their teachers step back into the role of active facilitators.

Integrating the eight essentials

As outlined in Chapter 1, the eight essentials for second language learning are Learner Autonomy, Social Nature of Learning, Integrated Curriculum, Focus on Meaning, Diversity, Thinking Skills, Alternative Assessment, and

Teachers as Co-learners. Each essential is summarized once more below for convenience:

- *Learner Autonomy*: this essential generally means our learners have greater choice over their own second language learning, both in terms of the content of that learning as well as processes they might use to accomplish the learning. In second language education as has been discussed in many of the preceding chapters, the use of small groups is one example of this, as is the use of self-assessment.
- *The Social Nature of Learning*: this essential emphasizes that learning a second language is not an isolated individual private activity (which many second language learners unfortunately still think is the case), but rather it is a social activity that encourages and really depends upon successful interaction with others. The popularity of the cooperative learning movement that has been discussed in many of the chapters of this book reflects this viewpoint.
- *Integrated curriculum*: this essential suggests that the connection between different strands of the curriculum should be emphasized, so that English as a second or foreign language is not seen as a stand-alone subject but is linked to all other subjects in the curriculum. Within second language education, text-based learning is one of many trends which reflects this essential, as it seeks to develop fluency in text types that can be used across the curriculum. An additional example can be seen in project work in language teaching and learning, which involves students in exploring issues outside of the language classroom. Both are discussed in detail in various chapters of this book.
- *Focus on Meaning*: in this essential meaning is viewed as the catalyst for real learning. Within second language learning, content-based teaching, for example, reflects this essential, as it seeks to make the exploration of meaning through content the main focus of language learning activities.
- *Diversity*: this essential urges that teachers not forget that all our students are different, and that these differences can be positive for second language learners, because, for instance, they learn in different ways and thus have different strengths. Second language teaching then should take these differences into account and use them for a positive outcome rather than try to force students into a single way of learning. In other words, second language teachers must gauge their students' learning styles while also emphasizing the implementation of different learning and communication strategies.
- *Thinking Skills*: this essential maintains that learning a second language should serve as a means of developing higher-order Thinking Skills, also known as critical and creative thinking, and not just listen and repeat. Thus, second language students do not learn language for its own sake but in order to develop and apply their Thinking Skills in situations that go beyond the language classroom into the community and the wider world.

- *Alternative Assessment*: this essential suggests that new forms of assessment are needed to compliment the more traditional modes of assessment, such as multiple-choice. Varied forms of assessment, such as students creating portfolios of all their work (e.g., all the drafts of a composition rather than just the final product) can be used to build up a comprehensive picture of what students can do in a second language rather than just giving them a final grade.
- *Teachers as Co-learners*: this essential suggests that teachers do not just teach and students learn; rather, teachers are viewed as facilitators who constantly try out alternatives, i.e., learning through doing. As a result, the classroom is not only a place where teachers blindly follow the teachers' manual and the higher-ups' dictates. In language teaching, this essential has led to an interest in reflective practice, action research, and other forms of classroom investigation

Throughout this book, we have urged our fellow second language educators to take a big picture approach to the changes in our profession. Although we presented eight essentials in separate chapters, we also pointed out that these essentials should not be taken as eight isolated parts of second language instruction and that in order to implement the CLT approach to second language education (or a "new paradigm" approach as we call it in this chapter – see above), all eight are and must be connected.

For example, the concept of *Learner Autonomy* fits with the overall change with a CLT approach to second language education because it emphasizes the role of the learner rather than the role of the teacher. It focuses on the process rather than the product and encourages students to develop their own purposes for learning and to see learning as a lifelong process.

The *Social Nature of Learning* emphasizes cooperation among all the stakeholders involved in second language learning. As with Learner Autonomy, the use of group activities places second language students at the center of attention, offering them one means of taking on more rights and responsibilities in their own learning. Additionally, cooperative learning acknowledges the place of affect in education, highlighting the importance of positive interdependence, where second language students feel support and belonging at the same time that they are motivated to try hard to assist the group in achieving results.

The essential *integrated curriculum* involves going from whole to part rather than from part to whole. For instance, under the traditional education model, students study a given historical period, e.g., the 19th century, in an isolated, decontextualized, atomistic way. In history class, they study key events, people, and movements. In science class, in another year or term, they discuss notable scientific discoveries. In language class, in yet another year or term they read literature from the period. Or, even if the 19th century is simultaneously dealt with in multiple classes, little or no effort is made to build learning links. Thus, students miss valuable opportunities for understanding context unless the curriculum is offered in an integrated manner where students can see the links for all the different subjects they are studying.

The essential *Focus on Meaning* takes a different view of learning from Behaviorist Psychology's emphasis on one size fitting all for learning and learners. In contrast, Socio-Cognitive Psychology stresses that people learn by chunking new information with existing knowledge and that meaning plays a key role in forming those chunks.

A key tenet of *Diversity* is that each second language learner is different and that effective language teaching needs to take these differences into account. As such, Diversity among our second language students is not seen as an obstacle, but as a real strength. The essential concept of *Thinking Skills* suggests that thinking is a process and the emphasis lies in the quality of that process rather than solely on the quality of the product resulting from that process. We also suggest that the essential of Thinking Skills can connect the language school with the community and world beyond. This attempt promotes the idea that second language learning is not a collection of lower-order rules and facts to be remembered and then regurgitated on exams, but that we learn in school in order to apply our knowledge toward making it in, and providing for, a better world.

Of course, the new paradigm from which flow these essential changes informs these changes in myriad ways. For example, an emphasis on meaning rather than form underlies many of the new assessment instruments, many Alternative Assessment methods, such as think aloud protocols, seek to investigate these processes, and the understanding of the *Social Nature of Learning* has led to the inclusion of peer assessment and to the use of group tasks in assessment, called *Alternative Assessment* in our eight essentials. Finally, under the "old paradigm" (as opposed to the "new paradigm" that we are suggesting in this book), second language teachers are seen as workers who need to be supervised by "experts," usually from universities and government agencies, the better to meet curriculum goals and lead students to perform according to prescribed schemes. Teaching, in this old paradigm view, can be broken into discrete skills that can be learned in isolation in an overall training approach to second language teaching education (Freeman, 1989). However, the new paradigm sees second language teaching and learning as social processes where the language students are active co-constructors of knowledge with their teachers. Thus, second language teachers are seen as co-learners and the *teacher as co-learner* is more of a facilitator and fellow learner alongside the students than a taskmaster who follows a prescribed instructional checklist.

Reflecting on the essentials

Finally, we suggest that each of the following questions be considered with other learner teachers and/or experienced teachers, so that you can all share your reflections. Perhaps you can form a teacher development group (see Farrell, 2007 for more on this topic and other topics related to reflecting on practice) and different members can take responsibility for leading the discussion on each of the questions below. This way, the person responsible for leading the discussion will arrange for a place to meet, make sure each participant has prepared for the meeting, make arrangements for who will record the ideas talked about during the meeting in case you may want to follow-up with another discussion or application of ideas discussed. In addition, the group and/or individuals may want to follow-up the discussions/reflections with an action research project on ideas and materials discussed in the book and/or at the group meetings. The idea is that the group as a whole should not just meet and leave it at that hoping for some inspiration to take place on its own; rather, we see this book as a beginning of your journey into your classroom as you reflect on what works best for you and your students. Here are a few questions to get you started but no doubt each teacher and each group of teachers will come up with their own questions based on their own needs and the needs of their students.

1. Within a CLT approach to second language education, Richards (2005) has suggested that in order for this approach to succeed, we need to consider the following ten core assumptions:

   a. Second language learning is best facilitated when students are interacting in meaningful communication.

   b. Tasks and activities have students negotiating meaning through meaningful interpersonal exchanges while at the same time noticing how the second language is used.

   c. Students process content that is purposeful, relevant, engaging, and interesting.

d. More than one language skill may be in use when communication is considered a holistic process.

e. Inductive style learning activities where students discover underlying rules of language best aid second language learning.

f. Errors are a natural and normal product of learning because second language learning is a gradual process.

g. Second language learners progress at different individual rates of learning and also have differing motivation levels and needs.

h. Learning and communication strategies when used effectively aid language learning.

i. The second language teacher creates the learning environment that facilitates language learning by creating opportunities for lots of practice in the language.

j. Collaboration and sharing within a classroom community is seen as central to language learning.

- Look at each of the assumptions (a) through (j) above, and then ask yourself:
  - o How many of these assumptions apply to your own classroom practices?
  - o How many of these assumptions are being adhered to by faculty and administrators of your language program and/or your school or institution?
  - o Choose one (or more) of the assumptions and detail how you have applied it in the past to your class, or how you intend to apply it in future.

2. In Chapter 1, we explain two reasons why the paradigm shift to CLT remains incomplete, despite CLT being the dominant paradigm for many years, at least in books, articles, and courses on how to teach second languages. The first of these two reasons is that the shift to CLT has been understood in a partial manner, with one essential or other CLT-linked concept focused on without seeing its fit to the larger picture. The second reason is that the shift has been implemented in a piecemeal manner. For instance, Learner Autonomy was honored via the establishment of a self-access center and the implementation of an extensive reading program. However, other essentials were ignored. For example, the Social Nature of Learning was left out, as students did their self-access work and their reading alone, without peer interaction. Similarly, the Alternative Assessment and the Thinking Skills essentials might have been neglected, with students still participating in only traditional forms of assessment and answering only lower-order thinking questions.

- Please describe how you do or how you could implement multiple essentials as a synergistic whole.

3. We have talked about eight possible essentials in English language education that we think are very important in order to properly implement Communicative Language Teaching (CLT). We have also suggested that these eight are inextricably linked to each other and cannot be treated as separate entities (although many are in different contexts).

- Can you think of any other essential that we may have missed but is also inextricably linked to a successful implementation to a CLT approach to English language education?

4. When we talk about change throughout this book we mean that English as a second/foreign language teachers should consider a change in the usual way of teaching second languages. We also maintain that change does not happen quickly in any field. For example, in the physical sciences, Kuhn (1970) has suggested that change in a scientific field does not occur as a step-by-step, cumulative process. Rather, he argued that new paradigms emerge as the result of tradition-shattering revolutions in the thinking of a particular professional community. These shifts involve the adoption of a new outlook on the part of researchers and others in that community. When a paradigm shift takes place, we see things from a different perspective as we focus on different aspects of the phenomena in our lives.

- What changes (if any) do you think has taken place in your thinking about teaching ESL/EFL as a result of reading the contents of this book? Try to explain the changes and why you have now come to think this way about ESL/EFL teaching. If you have not changed your thinking, please try to suggest reasons why you have not changed.

References

Alberta Human Rights Commission (1978).

Bailey, K. M. & Nunan, D. (Eds.) (1996). *Voices from the language classroom.* New York: Cambridge University Press.

Barnes, D. (1976). *From communication to curriculum.* Middlesex: Penguin.

Beckett, G. H. & Miller, P. C. (Eds.) (2006). *Project-based second and foreign language education: Past, present, and future.* Greenwich, CN: Information Age Publishing.

Benson, P. (2007). Autonomy in language teaching and learning. State of the art article. *Language Teaching, 40*(1), 21–40.

Beyer, B. K. (1984). Improving thinking skills: Defining the problem. *Phi Delta Kappan, 65*(7), 486–490.

Bloom, B. S. (Ed.) (1956). *Taxonomy of educational objectives: Classification of educational goals. Handbook 1. Cognitive domain.* New York: David McKay.

Breen, M. P. (2001). Navigating the discourse: On what is learned in the language classroom. In C. N. Candlin & N. Mercer (Eds.), *English language teaching in its social context* (pp. 306–322). London: Routledge. (First published in W. A. Renandya & G. M. Jacobs (Eds.) (1998). *Learners and language learning.* Anthology Series 39 (pp. 115–144). Singapore: SEAMEO Regional Language Centre.)

Breen, M. P. & Candlin, C. N. (1980). The essentials of a communicative curriculum in language teaching. *Applied Linguistics, 1*(2), 89–112.

Brinton, D. M., Snow, M. A., & Wesche, M. B. (1989). *Content-based second language instruction.* New York: Newbury House.

Brown, H. D. (2000). *Principles of language learning and teaching.* White Plains, NY: Addison Wesley Longman.

Bruce, C. D. & Ross, J. A. (2008). A model for increasing reform implementation and teacher efficacy: Teacher peer coaching in Grades 3 and 6 mathematics. *Canadian Journal of Education, 31*(2), 346–370.

Byrnes, D. A. & Kiger, G. (Eds.) (2005). *Common bonds: Anti-bias teaching in a diverse society* (3rd edn.). Olney, MD: Childhood Education International.

Cates, K. & Jacobs, G. M. (2006). Global issues projects in the English language classroom. In G. H. Beckett & P. C. Miller (Eds.), *Project-based second and foreign language education: Past, present, and future* (pp. 167–180). Greenwich, CN: Information Age Publishing.

Chalk, K. & Bizo, L. (2004). Specific praise improves on-tak behaviour and numeracy enjoyment: A study of year four pupils engaged in the numeracy hour. *Educational Psychology in Practice, 20*(4), 335–351.

Chamot, A. U. & O'Malley, J. M. (1994). *The CALLA Handbook: Implementing the Cognitive Academic Language Learning Approach.* Reading, MA: Addison-Wesley.

Collaborative for Academic, Social, and Emotional Learning. *SEL basics.* Retrieved December 28, 2008, from http://www.casel.org.

Compton, W. C. (2005). *An introduction to Positive Psychology.* Belmont, CA: Thomson/Wadworth.

Crandall, J. (Ed.) (1987). *ESL through content-area instruction.* Englewood Cliffs, NJ: Prentice Hall.

Crookes, G. & Lehner, A. (1998). Aspects of process in an ESL critical pedagogy teacher education course. *TESOL Quarterly, 32,* 319–328.

Cross, J. (2002). Noticing in SLA: Is it a valid concept? *TESL-EJ, 6*(3), A-2. Retrieved December 28, 2008, from http://www-writing.berkeley.edu/TESL-EJ/ej23/a2.html.

Csikszentmihalyi, M. (1990). *Flow: The psychology of optimal experience.* New York: Harper & Row.

Davies, M. A. (2005). Integrative studies: A teaching model to promote connective thinking. In J. S. Etim (Ed.), *Curriculum integration k-12: Theory and practice.* Lanham, MA: University Press of America, Inc.

—(2000). Learning . . . the beat goes on. *Childhood Education,* 76(3), 14–153.

Dunn, R., Beaudry, J. S., & Klaves, A. (1989). Survey on research on learning styles. *Educational Leadership,* 46(6), 50–58.

Early, M. (1990). Enabling first and second language learners in the classroom. *Language Arts, 67*(Oct.), 567–575.

Farrell, T. S. C. (2008). *Teaching reading to English language learners: A reflective guide.* Thousand Oaks, CA: Corwin Press.

—(2007). *Reflective language teaching: From research to practice.* London: Continuum Press.

—(2006). *Succeeding with English language learners: A guide for beginning teachers.* Thousand Oaks, CA: Corwin.

—(1999). Teachers talking about teaching: Creating conditions for reflection. *Teaching English as a Second or Foreign Language, 4*(2), 1–16 (in electronic format retrieved February 3, 2009, from http://www-writing.berkeley.edu/TESL-EJ/ej14/a1.html)

Feez, S. & Joyce, H. (1998). *Text-based syllabus design.* Sydney: National Centre for English Language Teaching and Research, Macquarie University.

Field, J. (2002). The Changing Face of Listening. In Jack. E. Richard & A. Renandya Willy (Eds.), *Methodology in language teaching: An anthology of current practice* (pp. 242–247). New York: Cambridge University Press.

Finocchiaro, M. & Brumfit, C. (1983). *The functional-notional approach.* Oxford: Oxford University Press.

Fisher, D. (2001). Cross age tutoring: Alternatives to the reading resource room for struggling adolescent readers. *Journal of Instructional Psychology, 28*(4), 234–240.

Frankl, V. (1959). *Man's search for meaning.* Boston: Beacon Press.

Freeman, D. (1996). Redefining the relationship between research and what teachers know. In Kathleen M. Bailey and David Nunan (Eds.), *Voices from the language classroom: Qualitative research in second language education* (pp. 88–115). Cambridge, UK: Cambridge University Press.

—(1989). Teacher training, development, and decision making: A model of teaching and related strategies for language teacher education. *TESOL Quarterly, 23,* 27–45.

Freeman, D. & Richards, J. C. (Eds.) (1996). *Teacher learning in language teaching.* New York: Cambridge University Press.

Freire, P. (1970). *Pedagogy of the oppressed.* New York: Seabury.

Fullan, M. (2008). *The six secrets of change: What the best leaders do to help their organizations survive and thrive.* San Francisco: Jossey Bass.

Gardner, H. (2006). *Multiple intelligences: New horizons.* New York: Basic Books.

—(1999). *Intelligence reframed: Multiple intelligences for the 21st century.* New York: Basic Books.

Gass, R. (1986). Earth is our mother. On Humanity (cassette), cited in Davies, M. A. (2000). Learning . . . the beat goes on. *Childhood Education, 76*(3), 14–153.

Gibbs, J. (2006). *Reaching all by creating Tribes learning communities.* Windsor, CA: CenterSource Systems.

Gidley, M. (1981). *Kopet: A Documentary Narrative of Chief Joseph's Last Years.* Seattle: U of Washington Press.

Gillies, R. M. (2007). *Cooperative learning: Integrating theory and practice.* Thousand Oaks, CA: Sage Publications.

Glasgow, N. & Farrell, T. S. C. (2007). *What successful literacy teachers do: 70 research-based strategies for teachers, reading coaches, and instructional planners.* Thousand Oaks, CA: Corwin Press.

Goleman, D. (2005). *Emotional intelligence.* New York: Bantam Books.

Gottlieb, M. (2006). *Assessing English language learners: Bridges from language proficiency to academic achievement.* Thousand Oaks, CA: Corwin Press.

Gregorc, A. F. (1979). Learning/teaching styles: Potent forces behind them. *Educational Leadership, 5,* 234–237.

Halliday, M. A. K. & Matthiessen, C. M. I. M. (1999). *Construing experience through meaning: A language-based approach to cognition.* London: Cassell.

Heath, S. B. (1983). *Ways with words: Language, life and work in communities and classrooms.* Cambridge: CUP.

Hicks, J. (2007). Students' view of cooperative learning and group testing. *Radiologic Technology, 78,* 275–283.

Hmelo-Silver, C. E. & Barrows, H. S. (2006). Goals and strategies of a problem-based learning facilitator. *Interdisciplinary Journal of Problem-based Learning, 1,* 21–39.

Holliday, A. (1991). From materials development to staff development: An informed change in direction in an EFL project. *System, 19*(3), 301–308.

Hymes, D. (1972). On communicative competence. In J. B. Pride & J. Holmes (Eds.), *Sociolinguistics* (pp. 269–293). Harmondsworth: Penguin.

Jacobs, G. M. & Farrell, T. S. C. (2003). Understanding and Implementing the CLT (Communicative Language Teaching) Paradigm. *RELC Journal, 34*(1), 5–30.

—(2001). Paradigm shift: Understanding and implementing change in second language education. *TESL-EJ, 5*(1). Retrieved September 12, 2009, from http://www.kyoto-su.ac.jp/information/tesl-ej/ej17/toc.html.

Jacobs, G. M. & Small, J. (2003, April). Combining dictogloss and cooperative learning to promote language learning. *The Reading Matrix, 3*(1). Retrieved February 3, 2009, from http://www.readingmatrix.com/articles/jacobs_small.

Jacobs, G. M., Power, M. A., & Loh, W. I. (2002). *The teacher's sourcebook for cooperative learning: Practical techniques, basic principles, and frequently asked questions.* Thousand Oaks, CA: Corwin Press.

Jensen, E. (2008). *Brain-based learning: The new paradigm of teaching* (2nd edn.). Thousand Oaks, CA: Corwin Press.

Johnson, D. W. & Johnson, F. P. (2009). *Joining together: Group theory and group skills.* Upper Saddle River, NJ: Pearson Education.

—(1999). *Learning together and alone* (4th edn.). Boston: Allyn and Bacon.

Kearney, P. (1993). *Cooperative learning techniques.* Hobart, Tasmania: Artemis Publishing.

Kecskes, K. (Ed.) (2006). *Engaging departments: Moving faculty culture from private to public, individual to collective focus for the common good.* Bolton, MA: Anker Publications.

Kuhn, T. S. (1970). *The structure of scientific revolutions* (2nd edn.). Chicago: University of Chicago Press.

Kweon, S. & Kim, H. (2008). Beyond raw frequency: Incidental vocabulary acquisition in extensive reading. *Reading in a Foreign Language, 20*(2), 191–215.

Lambros, A. (2004). *Problem-based learning in middle and high school classrooms: A teacher's guide to implementation.* Thousand Oaks, CA: Corwin Press.

Lee, M. J. W., Mcloughlin, C., & Chan, A. (2008). Talk the talk: Learner-generated podcasts as catalysts for knowledge creation. *British Journal of Educational Technology, 39*(3), 501–521.

Lewin, K. (1951). *Field theory in social science: Selected theoretical papers.* New York: Harper & Row.

Long, M. H. (1997). Authenticity and learning potential in L2 classroom discourse. In G. M. Jacobs (Ed.), *Language classrooms of tomorrow: Issues and responses* (pp. 148–169). Singapore: SEAMEO Regional Language Centre.

—(1991). Focus on form: A design feature in language teaching methodology. In K. de Bot, R. Ginsberg, & C. Kramsch (Eds.), *Foreign language research in cross-cultural perspective* (pp. 196–221). Cambridge: Cambridge University Press.

Long, M. H. & Crookes, G. (1992). Three approaches to task-based syllabus design. *TESOL Quarterly, 19*, 207–227.

Loporchio, A. F. (2006). *The hidden curriculum: Life in the public schools.* New York: Vantage Press.

Malcolm, I. (1996). A man of language. In G. M. Jacobs & B. R. S. Rajan (Eds.), *Who is the most talkative of them all: Stories for language teacher education* (pp. 31–33). Singapore: SEAMEO Regional Language Centre.

Nation, I. S. P. (2008). *Teaching ESL/EFL reading and writing.* New York: Routledge.

Neville, D. O. & Britt, D. W. (2007). A Problem Based Learning approach to integrating foreign language into Engineering. *Foreign Language Annals, 40*(2), 226–246.

Nowlan, A. G. P. (2008). Motivation and learner autonomy: Activities to encourage independent study. *The Internet TESL Journal, 19*(10). Retrieved January 2, 2009, from http://iteslj.org/Techniques/Nowlan-Autonomy.html.

Nunan, D. (2004). *Task-based language teaching.* Cambridge: Cambridge University Press.

Ogle, D. (1989). KWL: A teaching model that develops active reading of expository text. *Reading Teacher, 39*, 546–570.

Oprandy, R. (1999). Jane Jacobs: Eyes on the city. In D. J. Mendelsohn (Ed.), *Expanding our vision* (pp. 41–59). Toronto: Oxford University Press.

Pagel, J. W. (2002). Learner autonomy in a cooperative learning situation. *Kitasato Review: Journal of Liberal Arts and Sciences, 7*, 11–25.

Paul, R. W. & Elder, L. (2006). *Critical thinking: Tools for taking charge of your learning and your life* (2nd edn.). Upper Saddle River, NJ: Pearson/Prentice Hall.

Porter, H. (2008). *Mentoring new teachers* (3rd edn.). Thousand Oaks, CA: Corwin Press.

Powell, R. G. & Caseau, D. (2004). *Classroom communication and diversity: Enhancing instructional practice.* Mahwah, NJ: Lawrence Erlbaum.

Rea, S. (2001). Portfolios and process writing: A practical approach. *The Internet TESL Journal, 7*(6). Retrieved January 20, 2009, from http://iteslj.org/Tehniques/Rea-Portfolios.html.

Ribe, R. & Vidal, N. (1993). *Project work: Step by step.* Oxford: Heinemann.

Richards, J. C. (2005). *Communicative language teaching.* Singapore: SEAMEO, RELC.

Richards, J. C. & Farrell, T. S. C. (2005). *Professional development for language teachers.* New York: Cambridge University Press.

Richards, J. C. & Rodgers, T. S. (2001). *Approaches and methods in language teaching* (2nd edn.). Cambridge: Cambridge University Press.

Rivers, W. P. (2001). Autonomy at all costs: An ethnography of metacognitive self-assessment and self-management among experienced language learners. *The Modern Language Journal, 85*, 279–290.

—(1976). *Speaking in many tongues: Essays in foreign language teaching* (2nd edn.). Rowley, MA: Newbury House.

Robinson, P. (1980). *ESP (English for Specific Purposes).* Oxford: Pergamon.

Roehlkepartain, E. C. (2009). *Service-learning in community-based organizations: A practical guide to starting and sustaining high-quality programs.* Scotts Valley, CA: National Service-Learning Clearinghouse.

Schrum, J. & Glissan, E. (2000). *Teacher's handbook: Contextualized language instruction* (2nd edn.). Boston: Heinle & Heinle.

Scriven, M. & Paul, R. (1987, Summer). *Critical thinking as defined by the National Council for Excellence in Critical Thinking.* Statement at the 8th Annual International Conference on Critical Thinking and Education Reform.

Senge, P. (Ed.) (2000). *Schools that learn: A fieldbook for teachers, administrators, parents, and everyone who cares about education.* New York: Doubleday.

Slavin, R. E. (1995). *Cooperative learning: Theory, research, and practice* (2nd edn.). Boston, MA: Allyn and Bacon.

Sleeter, C., Torres, M., & Laughlin, M. (2004). Scaffolding conscientization in teacher education through teacher inquiry. *Teacher Education Quarterly. 31*(1), 81–96.

Stiggins, R. J. (2007). *Classroom assessment for student learning: Doing it right – using it well.* Upper Saddle River, NJ: Pearson Education.

Swain, M. (1999). Integrating language and content teaching through collaborative tasks. In W. A. Renandya & C. S. Ward (Eds.), *Language teaching: New insights for the language teacher* (pp. 125–147). Singapore: Regional Language Centre.

Tan, I. G.-C., Sharan, S., & Lee, C. K.-E. (2006). *Group investigation and student learning: An experiment in Singapore schools.* Singapore: Marshall Cavendish.

Vandrick, S. (1999, February/March). Who's afraid of critical and feminist pedagogies? *TESOL Matters, 9*(1), 9.

Voght, G. M. (2000). New paradigms for U. S. higher education in the twenty-first century. *Foreign Language Annals, 33,* 269–277.

Vygotsky, L. S. (1978). *Mind in society* (ed. by M. Cole, V. John-Steiner, S. Scribner, and E. Souberman). Cambridge, MA: Harvard University Press.

Wheatley, M. J. (2006). *Leadership and the new science: Discovering order in a chaotic world* (3rd edn.). San Francisco: Berrett-Koehler.

Wiggins, G. (1998). *Educative assessment: Designing assessments to inform and improve student performance.* San Francisco: Jossey-Bass.

Wilhelm, K. H. (2006). Teaching, practicing, and celebrating a cooperative learning model. In S. G. McCafferty, G. M. Jacobs, & Idding, A. C. D. (Eds.), *Cooperative learning and second language teaching* (pp. 153–176). New York: Cambridge University Press.

www.etherpad.com. Retrieved February 3, 2009.

Yeigh, T. (2008). Quality teaching & professional learning: Uncritical reflections of a critical friend. *Australian Journal of Teacher Education, 33*(2), 1–15.

Zukav, G. (2001). *The dancing wu li masters: An overview of the new physics.* New York: Perennial Classics.

Index

NOTE: Page references in *italics* refer to figures and tables; page references in **bold** include a vignette.